PRAYERS THAT OUTWIT THE ENEMY

Chuck has revealed the importance and power of prayer in *Prayers That Outwit the Enemy* by exposing the enemy and his tactics. I recommend this book for any believer who has found his or her prayer time to be lacking the presence of God.

JOHN BEVERE

AUTHOR, *DRAWING NEAR* AND *A HEART ABLAZE*
COFOUNDER, JOHN BEVERE MINISTRIES
SPEAKER, MESSENGER INTERNATIONAL

There is one thing that I guarantee will happen when you begin reading this book: You will want to stop and pray, and perhaps unlearn how to pray. We are indebted to my good friend Chuck Pierce, one of the most significant prophetic voices to the nations for this hour. He, indeed, is a powerful servant of the Lord who is used mightily to pull down strongholds and gain places of intercession for the glory of God. *Prayers That Outwit the Enemy* is a lifelong learning manual to keep with you at all times, right alongside your Bible, as you pray. Thanks, Chuck, for being faithful to feed us, stimulate us and provoke us to pray. It is time for the saints to outwit their enemy.

DR. MARK J. CHIRONNA

THE MASTER'S TOUCH INTERNATIONAL CHURCH
ORLANDO, FLORIDA

Chuck Pierce has emerged as a credible voice to this generation with strategic insight. His book provides prayer secrets that will unleash the power of God to accomplish the heavenly mandates dawning in this hour. Life in the Spirit is a journey of intimacy, prayer and Christlike character. *Prayers That Outwit the Enemy* is a great tool in this endeavor.

PAUL KEITH DAVIS

AUTHOR, *THRONES OF OUR SOUL*
CONFERENCE SPEAKER
FOUNDER, WHITE DOVE MINISTRIES

There are many books available on spiritual warfare, and most of them mention our God-given weapons. However, none of them is like this book. *Prayers That Outwit the Enemy* will lift our weaponry from a shotgun level to a machine gun level. Read this book and experience new dimensions of spiritual power!

C. PETER WAGNER

AUTHOR, *CHANGING CHURCH* AND *ACTS OF THE HOLY SPIRIT*
CHANCELLOR, WAGNER LEADERSHIP INSTITUTE

PRAYERS THAT OUTWIT THE ENEMY

CHUCK D. PIERCE
REBECCA WAGNER SYTSEMA

Regal

From Gospel Light
Ventura, California, U.S.A.

PUBLISHED BY REGAL BOOKS
FROM GOSPEL LIGHT
VENTURA, CALIFORNIA, U.S.A.
PRINTED IN THE U.S.A.

Regal Books is a ministry of Gospel Light, a Christian publisher dedicated to serving the local church. We believe God's vision for Gospel Light is to provide church leaders with biblical, user-friendly materials that will help them evangelize, disciple and minister to children, youth and families.

It is our prayer that this Regal book will help you discover biblical truth for your own life and help you meet the needs of others. May God richly bless you.

For a free catalog of resources from Regal Books/Gospel Light, please call your Christian supplier or contact us at 1-800-4-GOSPEL *or* www.regalbooks.com.

Cover design by Robert Williams
Interior design by Stephen Hahn

Appendix B, "Warring with a Prophetic Word" is reprinted from Chuck D. Pierce and Rebecca Wagner Sytsema, *The Best Is Yet Ahead*, Wagner Publications, 2001. Used by permission.

Library of Congress Cataloging-in-Publication Data
Pierce, Chuck D., 1953–
  Prayers that outwit the enemy / Chuck D. Pierce and Rebecca Wagner Sytsema.
    p. cm.
  Includes index.
  ISBN 0-8307-3162-8
  1. Spiritual warfare. 2. Prayer–Christianity. I. Sytsema, Rebecca Wagner. II. Title.
BV210.3.P54 2004
  235'.4–dc22   2004012468

2 3 4 5 6 7 8 9 10 11 12 13 14 15 / 10 09 08 07 06 05 04

Rights for publishing this book in other languages are contracted by Gospel Light Worldwide, the international nonprofit ministry of Gospel Light. Gospel Light Worldwide also provides publishing and technical assistance to international publishers dedicated to producing Sunday School and Vacation Bible School curricula and books in the languages of the world. For additional information, visit www.gospellightworldwide.org; write to Gospel Light Worldwide, P.O. Box 3875, Ventura, CA 93006; or send an e-mail to info@gospellightworldwide.org.

DEDICATION

With much love, we dedicate this book to our wonderful spouses, Pam Pierce and Jack Sytsema, who have consistently and strategically outwitted the enemy in our lives and homes.

CONTENTS

FOREWORD

By Dutch Sheets

Since Chuck Pierce first mentioned it to me, I have been fascinated by the title of this book, *Prayers That Outwit the Enemy*. I remember wishing I had thought of it first! Actually, I'm glad I didn't, because no one is as qualified to write this book as is Chuck. I do not hold this opinion based only on his theological excellence, intellectual brilliance or wise insights but also because I have marveled as I've watched him live out the truths he now writes about.

When Chuck has faced spiritual challenges and opportunities, time and again I have observed him receive clear strategies from the Holy Spirit, process them through sound biblical truth and apply them with practical wisdom. Moreover, as predictably as the sunrise, I watch the resulting fruit. Chuck has developed a remarkable ability to know when to act and when to wait. He knows how to discern what to do and what not to do. Though at times it looks like a sixth sense, I have come to understand that actually his heart and his mind are well trained and acutely sensitized to the Holy Spirit. He really is a modern-day son of Issachar: "Men who understood the times, with knowledge of what Israel should do" (1 Chron. 12:32, *NASB*). It is now our great opportunity to glean fruit once again from this Spirit-led man on a subject of paramount importance: prayers that outwit the enemy.

Genesis 3:1 says of Satan: "The serpent was more crafty than any beast." The Hebrew word translated here as "crafty" has in its etymology the concept of being bare or smooth. We still use the concept today when we speak of someone as being cunning in a bad sense, saying of them that they are slick, or perhaps that they are a smooth operator.

This same Hebrew word is sometimes translated as "wily," or "wilily." The New Testament, no doubt picking up on this concept, says of Satan's perverted yet subtle abilities: "Put on the whole armour of God, that ye may be able to stand against the *wiles* of the devil" (Eph: 6:11, *KJV*, emphasis added). The point is clear: Satan is far more dangerous to us as the wily serpent than as the roaring lion. He is far more effective with his slick craftiness than with his power or strength. The first verse of Martin Luther's hymn "A Mighty Fortress Is Our God" is very true:

> For still our ancient foe doth seek to work us woe;
> His craft and power are great, and, armed with cruel
>   hate,
> On earth is not his equal.

But as Chuck teaches us in this wonderful book, that isn't the end of the story. There is good news for us as we face our shrewd adversary: The wisdom of God infinitely supercedes the craftiness of the serpent! The Scriptures clearly state, "He captures the wise by their own shrewdness" (Job 5:13, *NASB*), and He "catches the wise in their craftiness" (1 Cor. 3:19, *NASB*). Placed in the context of the cross in order to prove His point, God confidently declares in 1 Corinthians 1:19, "For it is written, 'I will destroy the wisdom of the wise, and the cleverness of the clever I will set aside'" (*NASB*). Yes, He outwitted Satan at the cross and that is the ultimate proof that He will outwit him in every circumstance of our lives. Verses 2 and 3 of Luther's great hymn are equally true and poignant:

Did we in our own strength confide, our striving would
    be losing;
Were not the right Man on our side, the Man of God's
    own choosing:
Dost ask who that may be? Christ Jesus, it is He;
    Lord Sabaoth, His Name, from age to age the same,
And He must win the battle.

And though this world, with devils filled, should
    threaten to undo us,
We will not fear, for God hath willed His truth to tri-
    umph through us:
The Prince of Darkness grim, we tremble not for him;
His rage we can endure, for lo, his doom is sure,
One little word shall fell him.

Luther would have liked this book! He knew, when facing the evil one, how dependent we humans are on God's supernatural aid. He was also very confident of its availability. He understood our foe, but was impressed only by our God. So is Chuck, so am I, and so will you be after enjoying this great book.

A Note to Our Readers

We cowrote this book but write in a singular voice. Whenever a first-person pronoun is used (I, me, etc.), it is either Chuck speaking or both of us speaking. Whenever the illustration or point comes from Becky alone, we have identified it as such.

CHAPTER 1

CHECKMATE

The painting was eerie and disturbing—the kind not easily erased from one's memory. It hung on a wall inside a farmhouse somewhere outside Richmond, Virginia. Dinner had just been served when the chess master noticed. He was the guest of honor that night—sometime in the mid-1800s—but he could not help but stare at the image, almost speechless.

This particular piece of art depicted a chess match well under way. On one side of the board sat a man whose slumped shoulders and panicked eyes showed utter defeat. The look on his face left the viewer with the impression that the stakes surrounding this duel had been high—his very soul had been waged on the outcome. On the other side of the board was an awful and terrifying image of Mephistopheles—the legend of Faust who represents the spirit of the devil, the soul stealer. Mephistopheles's large figure was rising from his chair in obvious victory, gloating over the spoils he was ready to seize from this pitiful opponent. He was ready to shout, "Checkmate!"

The chess master's host was a preacher. No doubt on many occasions he had stood and looked intently into the hopeless and horrified eyes of the defeated man depicted in the painting

SATAN WILL TRY TO DECLARE CHECKMATE TIME AND TIME AGAIN, SEEKING TO CONVINCE US THAT HE HAS WON.

and pondered how many people in his own town lived with their souls overtaken by the devil. The chess master, on the other hand, focused on the board, intently calculating how the game had been played. He stared for a long time. So intrigued was the chess master that he set up his own prized chessboard and meticulously re-created the game shown in the painting.

The preacher and the other dinner guests, no doubt, were intrigued. "What are you doing?" they likely asked. The chess master most surely looked up from the chessboard with a gleam in his eyes. As legend has it, he then challenged the others to a game of chess. He would start severely handicapped, with his pieces placed in the position held by the young man in the painting who was on the brink of defeat. Whichever dinner guest would take the devil's side would seem to have the upper hand. At least one guest could not resist the temptation to beat the master at his own game and chose to side with Mephistopheles.

One version of this popular tale has the legendary 19th-century chess champion Paul Morphy declaring, "This artist has made a mistake! There is no checkmate. Satan has not won. See here? Look!" Pointing to the board, he drew a deep breath and loudly announced, "The king has one more move!"[1]

How true it is in our lives as well. Satan will try to declare checkmate time and time again, seeking to convince us that he has won and that there is no way out. But God, our King, has a destiny for each of our lives. Our destiny, our family's destiny and our territory's destiny are at the heart of any attack that the enemy launches against us. Satan knows that if our spirit ever comes alive to all God has, we will become a weapon in His hands, and we will have the authority to oppose evil with great force. When we know God's direction for our life, and allow Him to work out the gifting within us, we become a real and present threat to the enemy. That is why Satan will make strategic moves against us in order to stop us from accomplishing God's purposes.

But knowing that God has something greater and bigger planned for us is central to our gaining both the energy and the strategy to outwit our enemy. We can be assured that, as Satan launches his assaults against us and all may seem lost, the King has one more move!

THE GAME OF WAR

Many times we can learn a lot from games. In fact, I think that some games were inspired by God to teach us about the spiritual dynamic around us. Chess fits into this category. In his book *Chess: From First Moves to Checkmate*, Daniel King wrote,

> Chess is a game of war. You control one army and your opponent, the enemy, controls the other. The fate of your army depends entirely on your own skill. Most other games rely on chance—a move may be determined by a roll of the dice, or the turn of a card. But in chess there is no luck. You are entirely responsible for your own success or failure, and this is why chess can be one of the most satisfying of all games to win. . . . Before you make a move on the chessboard you must try to predict, as far as you can, how your opponent will react. In deciding what to play, you will need to use reason, memory, and logic combined with a dash of intuition and inspiration.[2]

Here is where I see that chess takes on a spiritual dimension. As we find ourselves engaged in war with the enemy, not only does God require us to yield our minds to His control, but He also gives us greater levels of spiritual intuition and inspiration. We will discuss both of these in greater detail throughout this book, but for now let's take a brief look at each aspect.

Within every one of us, men and women alike, there is a function called intuition. Once we have been saved and our spirit is connected back with its maker and creator, our intuition is then activated in new dimensions and becomes much sharper. Stimulated by the Holy Spirit within us, intuition includes God-given wisdom, knowledge, discernment and other similar supernatural understanding of what is going on around us. Our intuition, therefore, helps us to understand the moves the enemy makes against us, what he is likely to do next and how we can make strategic moves that both thwart his plans and advance us toward victory. Intuition, guided by the Holy Spirit, gives us the ability to overcome our enemy.

Inspiration is another issue. It is the very core of faith. When we have faith deep within our spirit, we are inspired. If we are inspired, we have been breathed upon or infused with life. This breath of life causes us to be guided, to be motivated and to seek out the communication with God that we need in order to bring divine influence into our lives and actions. In order to stay the course for the long haul without growing weary, we need to have divine inspiration that refreshes, renews and provides us with hope—especially in those times when the enemy tries to wrongly convince us that he has won. Inspiration is that which arises within us to shout, "The King has one more move!"

THE ROLE WE EACH PLAY

King writes further about chess, but he could be setting up my next point about the spiritual realm.

> It has been claimed that there are more possible moves on the chessboard than there are atoms in the universe. This helps account for the game's popularity through the ages. Chess has never been "solved." Even in today's computer age, it remains as complex and fascinating as it must have been when it emerged in India, almost 1,500 years ago.[3]

We can apply the same concept to our spiritual life. It is very much like a chess game. There are an infinite number of possible moves that can turn the game in this or that direction. The

Lord's leading in our lives is, therefore, essential. This applies both to individual believers and to the corporate Body of Christ.

Let's continue to use the analogy of the chess game as we see where each of us fits in the Body of Christ. When playing a game of chess, we need to know each piece and its function. Let's again turn to King for an explanation of how it works in chess.

> The value of each piece is based on its power on the board. Remembering these values will help you decide which pieces to exchange, and which pieces to keep.[4]

We all have value in the eyes of the Lord. Each one of us has a different place to stand, different gifts and a different measure of faith, but we all have value.

> O LORD, You have searched me and known me . . . For you formed my inward parts; You covered me in my mother's womb. I will praise You for I am fearfully and wonderfully made. . . . My frame was not hidden from You when I was made in secret. . . . Your eyes saw my substance, being yet unformed. And in Your book they all were written, the days fashioned for me, when as yet there were none of them (Ps. 139:1,13-16).

In other words, God valued you enough to make you!

In chess, the queen, with its ability to move like a bishop and a rook, is by far the most powerful piece on the board. When the queen is in the center of the board, it exercises extraordinary power. The queen's influence stretches from one side of the board to the other. The queen can move to any square. If the queen is lost, the chances of winning the game become greatly reduced.

The rook (also known as the castle) is another strategic piece, although unable to utilize its full power at the beginning of a game. A rook can only move up and down or side to side; it cannot leap because it is hemmed in. The bishop and the knight are also important, but not as versatile. These pieces are all useful guides when we are making strategic decisions in a heated battle for the board.

EACH ONE OF US HAS A DIFFERENT PLACE TO STAND, DIFFERENT GIFTS AND A DIFFERENT MEASURE OF FAITH, BUT WE ALL HAVE VALUE.

Then of course there is the pawn. Even though the pawn seems lowly, it protects the other pieces. At times, it is sacrificed to gain valuable positioning for future moves. Ordinary and humble as it may seem, the pawn has incredible potential because, if it reaches the far side of the board, it can be exchanged for a queen, bishop, knight or rook. The pawn is like you! You were born with great potential. You might go through some hard times that seem very sacrificial, but you can cross over and make it to the other side. It is in the persevering and overcoming that the fullness of your potential can be recognized!

THE END OF THE GAME

> The king is the most important piece on the chessboard. The whole game revolves around the struggle to trap the king. This is called checkmate. Lose this piece and you lose the game, so it is vital to keep the king as secure as possible.[5]

Once we come into covenant with a holy God and He inhabits our life and dwells within us, our opponent, the devil, must devise strategies to stop the King from being recognized and established within us.

> Checkmating your opponent's king is the ultimate aim in a chess game. The term comes from the ancient Persian "Shah mat," meaning "the king is defeated." You have to threaten the enemy king with one of your pieces so that it is unable to move and escape capture. A checkmate usually occurs when one side's forces—or "army"—are overwhelmingly superior, or by a direct and unexpected assault on the king.[6]

The enemy of our soul will threaten us constantly. He will devise plans to trap us. Though our adversary at times seems overwhelmingly superior, God in us, the hope of glory, will always give us a way to escape.

King explains how checkmate is different from checking.

> [Checking] occurs when the king is attacked by a piece, but can still escape. In other words, it is not necessarily fatal. Don't panic if your opponent suddenly thumps down a piece and cries "check." It does not end the game,

and it does not always benefit your opponent. So what exactly is the point of checking? A check can help you gain time. Checking can drive the enemy king to a weak square making it vulnerable to further attack.[7]

THOUGH OUR ADVERSARY AT TIMES SEEMS OVERWHELMINGLY SUPERIOR, GOD IN US, THE HOPE OF GLORY, WILL ALWAYS GIVE US A WAY TO ESCAPE.

Many of us are thrown off when the enemy checks us. Be willing to keep going and know that, in reality, you have a way to escape! In Matthew 24:13 we find, "But he that shall endure unto the end, the same shall be saved" (*KJV*). When the enemy checks you or tries to convince you that the game is over, you can be the one to remind him that "the King has one more move!" And as you move forward and outwit the enemy, you will be the one who ultimately shouts, "Checkmate!"

REVELATION

In order to get to that place of declaring "Checkmate!" we must learn to live in the revelation of the Lord. Why? Because Satan, the father of lies, works to keep us in darkness and tries to keep us believing his lies, much like the poor man in the painting who believed the chess game was over. He was ready to relinquish his soul to the enemy because he believed a well-disguised lie. Satan tries to blind our minds in many ways in order to deceive us. He tries to convince us with wrong thoughts about God. He attempts to develop prejudices of all kinds within us that build walls that darken our understanding. He attempts to infiltrate us with philosophies of this world that create wrong belief systems. He attempts to erect false reasoning in order to occupy our thoughts with earthly things. He tries to overwhelm us with the cares and pleasures of this world.

Satan loves to mix his lies with partial truth. That is what makes the lies seem so believable. It is also why we need revelation. I like what Paul Keith Davis wrote in *Engaging the Revelatory Realm of Heaven.*

> Currently the Lord is allowing many in the Church to see things taking place in the second Heaven as well as portions of His perfect plan in the third Heaven. The enemy would have people believe all is well, by calling good things as "evil" and base or foolish things as "good." Presently a deceptive voice seeks to find an outlet to hinder the preparation of God's people for the end-time battle.[8]

"Revelation" means to manifest, to make clear, to show forth, to unfold, to explain by narration, to instruct, to admonish, to warn or to give an answer to a question. When God speaks to us, He brings one or more of these aspects of revelation so that the eyes of our minds may be enlightened to who He is. Throughout history, God has actively disclosed Himself to humanity. God has not wavered in His desire that we also understand Him. He continues to reveal His power, His glory, His nature, His character, His will, His ways, His plans and His strategies to His people today.

Revelation from God has three important functions in our lives.

1. **Revelation causes obscure things to become clear.** Jeremiah 33:3 in *The Amplified Bible* reads, "Call to Me and I will answer you and show you great and mighty things, fenced in and hidden, which you do not know (do not distinguish and recognize, have knowledge of and understand)."

2. **Revelation brings hidden things to light.** One important definition of "revelation" is *apocalypse*, which means to unveil or reveal something that is hidden so that it may be seen and known for what it is.

3. **Revelation gives us signs that point us to our path of destiny.** We need revelation in order to know God's will for our lives and, as we come into agreement with His will, how to walk it out. By this we see that revelation is not a one-time deal. We need fresh revelation on a continual basis to keep moving forward in God's plan and timing, and to keep our minds from the enemy's deceptions.

These three functions of revelation help us understand the why, but an even bigger question is, How? Let's look at Ephesians 1:20-23:

Which He worked in Christ when He raised Him from the

dead and seated Him at His right hand in the heavenly places, far above all principality and power and might and dominion, and every name that is named, not only in this age but also in that which is to come. And He put all things under His feet, and gave Him to be head over all things to the church, which is His body, the fullness of Him who fills all in all.

This passage shows us that Jesus is able to defeat the enemy's structures in our lives from His position as head because all things are under His feet. Because Jesus is head, we need to think the way He thinks and put on the mind of Christ (see 1 Cor. 2:16).

The problem is that our minds are naturally at enmity with God because of our flesh. We must put on the mind of Christ

WE NEED TO THINK THE WAY JESUS THINKS AND PUT ON THE MIND OF CHRIST.

so that the Spirit of wisdom and revelation is activated in our lives. To do this, we need to believe that God will show us new revelation in a way that we, individually, can receive. The first important step in gaining revelation, therefore, is to trust that God has a way to communicate it to us. The next step is being open to and aware of what God is saying. The third step is to enter into a new dimension of faith, which we will discuss more in chapter 7.

It is one thing to decide that we want to enter into this new dimension, but it is quite another to get there. We need the Holy Spirit to help us through this process. Because revelation does not come through our own strength, we have to stay in intimate contact with God in order to gain revelation from Him and eventually yell "Checkmate!" against the enemy. Revelation leads us to wisdom, and wisdom gives us strategy. Strategy overthrows Satan's plans. But if we don't stay close to God, we won't have clear revelation. We must continue our dialogue with Him. Once we're dialoging in intimacy with God, He will give us three important revelations.

1. **He reveals Himself to us.** Unless we truly know who God is, we will never have what we need to outwit the devil. Our foundation will be shaky, and we will not enter into the level of faith that we need to conquer our enemy. When we have faith we are saying that we know God will do what He has promised to do. But unless we have a glimpse of who He really is, our faith will not have an opportunity to arise with us. We need to know God and His faithfulness to His promises in order to see how committed He is to overthrowing the enemy in our personal situations.

2. **He will reveal who you are in Him.** As we draw close to God, we begin to understand why He has made us. That is what the hope of His calling is all about (see Eph. 1:18). Hope is an important element for moving forward with confidence. As

God reveals who we are and what our calling is, we gain hope for our future. The enemy loves to come against our hope, and usually does so with trauma and grief in our lives. Trauma and grief are diametrically opposed to hope, and can cause us to lose our insight into God's identity for us. Of course, there are events and seasons in our lives that will naturally bring us into feelings of trauma and grief. If during such seasons we are able to remain intimate with the Lord, these natural feelings will not be able to overtake our spirits and souls in such a way that they become instruments in the hands of the enemy who wants to destroy our future.

3. **He will reveal who our enemy is and how he is working against us.** If we are to outwit the devil, we need to know the devil. This may be a very new thought for many who have somehow come to believe that paying any attention to the devil is the same as coming into agreement with him. That is not so. Every successful war strategy that has ever been launched in history has included both reconnaissance and an understanding of how the enemy thinks and what he is likely to do. In this case, we need to allow the Lord to be our reconnaissance, and we need to actively seek both wisdom and strategy from Him. As we learn more about our enemy, we need to remember that there is great truth in 1 John 4:4: "You are of God, little children, and have overcome them, because He who is in you is greater than he who is in the world."

PRAYER

We must rise up now and become intimate with God. The only way to do that is to spend time communing with Him in prayer. Prayer is dialogue. If we dialogue with God, we will overcome our enemy. The enemy cannot overcome God. That is why this book is called *Prayers That Outwit the Enemy*. As we utilize the different forms of prayer described in this book, we will become more intimate with God. Moreover, as we become more intimate with God, we'll also come to know the workings of the devil in our midst.

It is time for us to recover our losses! It is time for Satan to release our supply! It is time for a release of strength! It is time for God's people to invade Satan's territory and to advance His kingdom on Earth.

Our prayer for you in days ahead is that you will become connected to God's Spirit of wisdom and revelation so that you will have all that you need to outwit and checkmate the devil in your life, your family and your territory.

Notes

1. Through the years variations of this story have been told and pastors often use it as an illustration. It appears to have at least some validity and, for our purposes, works to illustrate our point. The painting in the story is likely one created by master artist Friedrich Moritz Auguste Retzsch (1779-1857). It depicts a young man playing chess against Mephistopheles, who has the upper hand. Though some claim that Bobby Fischer was the chess champion who re-created the game, Paul Morphy was more likely the man. In the November/December issue of *Virginia Chess*, John T. Campbell recounts how he located the actual Retzsch lithograph that had hung in the home of a nineteenth-century pastor named A. A. Howison. The pastor's descendants still possess the painting and, though the account is somewhat different from what we have presented, they continue to pass down from generation to generation memories of the night the chess champion came to dinner.

2. Daniel King, *Chess: From First Moves to Checkmate* (New York: Kingfisher, 2000), p. 6.
3. Ibid., p. 6.
4. Ibid., p. 21.
5. Ibid., p. 12.
6. Ibid., p. 20.
7. Ibid., pp. 20-21.
8. Paul Keith Davis, *Engaging the Revelatory Realm of Heaven* (North Sutton, NH: Streams Publications, 2003), p. 75.

CHAPTER 2

KNOW THE ENEMY

One night I was at home watching a movie with my kids. It was a good movie about an unconventional musician who takes an assignment as a substitute teacher in a very conventional prep school. What caught my ear was when I heard the teacher defining "the man" to these kids. He defined "the man" as an individual who has such influence or authority in your life that your freedom becomes hindered and controlled.

How interesting. That sounds like Isaiah's definition of Lucifer. After describing Satan's boasting and his eventual fall, Isaiah 14:16 reads, "Those who see you will gaze at you, and

consider you, saying: 'Is this *the man* who made the earth tremble, who shook kingdoms?'" (emphasis added). We see in the
Bible that there are many instances of "the man." Pharaoh was
"the man." The Amalekites were "the man." Jezebel and Ahab
formed a team to become "the man." In the New Testament, we
find Jesus dealing with "the man" and calling him Satan.

KNOW THE ENEMY BY SIGHT

I believe that it is very important to know the overall purpose of
a thing. In other words, why do we do what we do? Why do we
try to understand something? First John 3:8 clears up a lot about
the enemy: "He who sins is of the devil, for the devil has sinned
from the beginning. For this purpose the Son of God was manifested, that He might destroy the works of the devil."

Every time we sin, who is behind it? The devil. Some may
question this statement, but we must remember that he is the
father of all lies and author of all sin. When our flesh aligns itself
to do the will of the enemy, we have come into communion with
"the man" in our life. He will eventually dominate us.

As a teenager, I strayed from the Lord. I had lived through
several terrible years. My family was torn apart as my father sank
deep into gambling and many other sinful patterns. This season
culminated with my father's death. When I was 18, I became very
ill and ended up in the hospital for some time. During that time
I began to reconnect with God. I asked the Lord why I was drawn
to do the things I hated to do. God showed me that even though
I belonged to Him, the devil was superimposed over my body,
and He said, "This is the controlling force in your life, not Me."
I called upon the Lord who was in me, and I said, "You are
greater in me than that which is superimposed over me. If You

will rise up over me, the devil will have to leave me." In those days I knew nothing about the Bible, much less deliverance. But when I called out, the Spirit of God came down in that hospital room and visited me for three days.

While there the Lord said to me, "It wasn't your father who ruined your family. It was the devil. Your father came into agreement with him. Therefore, all the prosperity that I had planned

WE CAN'T TRULY OUTWIT THE DEVIL UNTIL WE HAVE AN UNDERSTANDING OF WHO HE IS AND HOW HE OPERATES.

for you as a family, Satan seized through sin, and he is trying to keep it from coming to the next generation." I knew right then that I had a choice. I could rise up and begin to become a student of God and a student of the Holy Spirit, or I could go the way of my earthly father.

During this time, the Holy Spirit became tangible to me. There has to come a time when the Holy Spirit becomes real for each of us. Once that happens, we are propelled into warfare. If we have been taught that the Holy Spirit is released in us purely for our joy and comfort, we have only been taught part of the picture. He can keep us filled with joy. He can comfort us and He can teach us. But the Holy Spirit will also open our eyes to the dark world around us so that we are able to see how the enemy is working against us. We can't truly outwit the devil until we have an understanding of who he is and how he operates.

KNOW THE ENEMY BY NAME

In the Bible, particularly the New Testament, the devil is described in many ways. Here we also learn that he operates not only on Earth as a whole, but also in the lives of individuals. He opposes God's purposes on Earth and devises schemes to prevent God's people from entering into those purposes. He is not a creature in a red suit with horns; rather, he can be a deceiving angel of light. We know people by their names. Therefore, let's look at some of the names and terms the Bible uses to describe Satan.

1. **The dragon or the old serpent** (see Rev. 12:9; 20:2). The dragon or the serpent reveals a characteristic of the enemy that will war with the Church until the end. Jesus Christ defeated him fully at the Cross, but because we live in a time before the second coming of Christ when Satan's defeat will be complete, we too must arise and face this creature who continues to wreak havoc on Earth. We will be in enmity with the serpent until the end. He is clever, religious and filled with political strength and authority.

2. **A deceiver** (see Gen. 3). Satan came to Adam and Eve and deceived them. Basically he said to them, "God is holding back on you!" Once Adam and Eve believed the lie, Satan was able to attach himself to their desires and manipulate them into sin. Satan will

often deceive us in the same way by telling us that God is somehow holding back on us, and if we will do this or that, we will get whatever it is that God does not want us to have. If we buy into the lie, Satan can then lure us into sin that separates us from God's path for our life. The absolute truth is that God doesn't hold back on us! God loves us and wants the best for us. He has a path and a destiny that will add everything to us that we need (see Matt. 6:33). But we, just like Adam and Eve, can choose to be diverted from that path through sin and disobedience, and Satan knows it. Therefore, he will do whatever he can to deceive us into sinning.

3. **Our adversary** (see Num. 22:22). An adversary is one who opposes us. Satan opposes the work of God's chosen ones (see 1 Thess. 2:18). He opposes our faith. He knows that our devotion to God can overthrow his power in the territory where we have been positioned on Earth. The enemy is looking for ways to stop our faith from propelling us into God's full plan for our life. As more and more of God's servants arise, Satan's defeat becomes inevitable.

4. **A usurper** (see Gen. 3). When Satan disobeyed God, he moved in to usurp God's rightful place. Satan's downfall was that, before he was expelled from heaven, he had an inordinate desire for the angels to admire him. He, therefore, sought to exalt himself higher than God by usurping and betraying his creator. Satan has worked in the same way throughout the ages. He seeks ways of dethroning God in individuals' hearts and in territories. His pride causes him to both beguile and

seduce—traits that he has fully mastered.

5. **An accuser.** Notice that the moment God confronted Adam and Eve, they turned on each other (see
   Gen. 3:13). The sin that Satan drew them into
   caused an accusing spirit to rise up within them.
   Satan will always try to do the same with us by causing us to question our brothers and sisters in the
   Lord through false accusations spread by gossip; by
   causing us to accuse one another through our own
   anger or hurt; by causing false accusations to be
   launched against us; or by causing us to accuse ourselves with an ungodly spirit of condemnation. If
   God is bringing conviction to our heart, it will cause
   us to want to get right with God and move forward
   in His plan. But if an ungodly spirit of condemnation is coming against us, we will feel separated
   from God in a way that will seem irreparable; and we
   will turn aside from His path and go into various
   forms of self-destruction.

6. **A tempter** (see 1 Cor. 7:5). Satan loves to find our
   weaknesses. He can and will tempt us to fall into
   sinful patterns. Satan's goal is to cause us to fail
   and then deviate from God's path for our life.
   When we give in to his temptations, he is able to
   divert us and clothe us in shame, disgrace and condemnation. But we need to remember that even
   though he has the power to tempt us, he cannot
   force us to do his will. In fact, temptation offers us
   the possibility of choosing holiness over sin. James
   1:2 shows us that we can even count such things as
   joy. If we do not allow the tempter to overtake us,
   we can use his temptations to produce overcoming

faith in our lives, and we will be able to rejoice in his defeat!

7. **A legalist.** We see throughout the Bible that Satan tries to use the law to bind and restrict rather than bring the freedom of God. The Pharisees are a good example of how legalism can obscure God's true intent. Furthermore, as we will see a little further in this chapter, Satan works to change laws so that they align with sinful practices rather than with bringing God's righteousness to territories.

SATAN IS ALWAYS SEEN AS HOSTILE TO GOD AND IS WORKING TO OVERTHROW GOD'S PURPOSES.

8. **Supremely evil Beelzebub, "The Lord of the Flies"** (see Matt. 12:24,27). He is the prince of the devils (see 12:24). He controls elaborate, well-organized demonic structures that have been set up to exalt himself and further his purposes throughout the world.

9. **The prince of the power of the air** (see Eph. 2:2). His power is very great on this planet. He is always seen as hostile to God and is working to overthrow God's purposes. He works to rule entire societies,

and he attempts to fill the atmosphere (air) around us with his presence and influence.

10. **The prince of this world** (see John 12:31; 14:30). A prince is one who holds legal right to a kingdom. Satan exercises and maintains his legal right as prince through human sin and failures on Earth. He manipulates the structures of the world.

The above characteristics enable us to better know our enemy. By knowing his names and descriptions, we can detect his presence whenever he is around us.

KNOW THE ENEMY BY HIS ACTIONS

Just as we can know the enemy by his name, we can also identify him by his actions. Knowing how he acts helps us discern when he is in our midst.

1. **Satan has a discernible presence.** When we are walking with the Lord and being guided by the Holy Spirit, we are able to discern the presence of evil. It is almost as if all the hair on our arms will stand up when Satan or his forces are around. When this happens, we have come to know his presence. We know what's going on. Our spirit tells us that something isn't right. This discernment is a function of the wisdom that comes through the Holy Spirit.

2. **Satan will bind us to doctrines.** Satan is very religious and legalistic. Therefore, he creates structures that hold us in place through religious legalism. But let's be clear about this point. Religious

legalism is nothing more than superstition! Superstition says that if we do A, B and C, then we can expect D to occur. Or it says, if A occurs, then we need to do B, C and D in order to cancel out any bad effects of A. For instance, some may feel they have to leave their Bible open to a certain passage in their bedroom or else Satan will gain access. Others may think that they have to light a candle or burn incense to maintain the presence of God. Some fear actually saying the name of the devil or coming against him because they think that such acts are invitations for him to operate in their lives. The truth is that Satan already plots against each of us. These superstitious rituals are legalistic and come with demonic snares. If the Lord has someone do a prophetic act for a particular reason, that's one thing. There is freedom in that. But if people blindly follow rituals that they do not understand, there is no freedom in that because they are bound to that ritual instead of seeking fresh strategy from God.

3. **Satan is continually opposed to the gospel.** We see evidence of this throughout the Lord's ministry; Satan attempted to work through Jesus' followers. He hates those who carry the good news, and he connives to confuse and hinder anyone who is communicating God's redemptive plan.

4. **Satan searches for men and women who can be "taken captive by him"** (2 Tim. 2:26). He longs to seduce us from God's path and to control our wills.

5. **He is a "roaring lion, seeking whom he may devour"** (1 Pet. 5:8). He lurks and lies in wait to

ambush us on our path.

6. **He looks for opportune times.** When the period of testing in the wilderness had been completed for Jesus, the devil left Him "until an opportune time," which implies that the enemy would watch for his next opportunity (see Matt. 3:11). This is essential for us to understand. We defeat the enemy battle by battle. Even if we have won a victory against him, we need to remember that he will look for another opportunity to attack or oppose us.

7. **He changes laws.** Because he is a legalist, Satan must use laws and control entire political and social structures to benefit his plans. By doing so, he is able to obscure the absolute truth of God's righteousness and cause that which God abhors to seem almost benign. An example of this in the United States at the time of this writing is same-sex marriage. This is a huge debate in which Satan has diverted attention away from righteousness and toward the so-called rights of individuals to act in whatever way seems right to them. The push in many states to allow such marriages will ultimately produce legally sanctioned unions that are diametrically opposed to an absolute truth that God has set forth in both the Old Testament and the New Testament.

KNOW THE ENEMY'S LIMITATIONS

Despite looking at the power and intent of the enemy, we can't ever forget that he is a defeated enemy. Paul can say confidently, "The God of peace will crush Satan under your feet shortly"

(Rom. 16:20). Satan and the demonic forces have been defeated by the life, death and resurrection of Jesus Christ. In the end, Satan and his angels will be completely overcome. In fact, Jesus

SATAN AND THE DEMONIC FORCES HAVE BEEN DEFEATED BY THE LIFE, DEATH AND RESURRECTION OF JESUS CHRIST.

came into the world to "destroy the works of the devil" (1 John 3:8). The Cross was a decisive victory over Satan and Satan's host (see Col. 2:15). This victory insured that countless numbers would be delivered from the dominion of darkness and transferred to the kingdom of Christ (see Col. 1:13). But this is not just an end-time promise for when the clouds part and we see the Lord descend. We have promises of Satan's defeat in our lives today. We are the only ones who can allow him to become "the man" in our lives, but we, through the leading of the Holy Spirit, also have the authority to outwit his schemes and dethrone him!

ALWAYS PRAY

Keep praying and seeking the Lord and you will overcome your enemy! The Lord began to move in me in the late 1970s to renew and energize my prayer life. I found myself staying up late and praying. God gave me actual prayer assignments. He had me pray for individuals, for my Sunday School class, for our church, for my pastor and for the church staff. I prayed for the company at which I worked. I prayed for my family. I simply was enjoying communicating with the Lord and watching Him work.

One night after I had my prayer time, I went to bed. At 2:00 A.M., I was awakened and our dog was growling and getting into the bed with us. My wife, Pam, was awakened and startled as well. I felt a presence in our room. Pam described this presence as a slimy green vapor—it was at the end of our bed. I stood up on our bed and commanded this presence to leave our house. I knew that enemy was angry over my prayer becoming active. This evil force was hoping to deter me from getting to know the Lord better. It was if he was attempting to produce fear in me so I would stop praying. He knew that if I kept seeking the Lord with all my heart I would eventually be free and able to recognize and confront him in new ways to defeat his purposes.

I want to encourage you to not let the enemy create fear in you. Do not be afraid to understand the enemy's schemes, character and ways. Go all the way with the Lord. Keep gaining victory over the enemy's plan to control and ruin your life. Remember, one small word fells him, this "man" who would rob you of your joy and life.

When contending with "the man," I am reminded that we have The Man contending for us. I am often encouraged by remembering the words of the classic hymn *A Mighty Fortress Is Our God*.

Did we in our own strength confide, our striving would
    be losing,

Were not the right man on our side, the man of God's
   own choosing.
Dost ask who that may be? Christ Jesus, it is He—
Lord Sabaoth His name, from age to age the same,
And He must win the battle.

And though this world with devils filled, should threat-
   en to undo us,
We will not fear, for God hath willed, His truth to
   triumph through us.
The prince of darkness grim, we tremble not for him—
His rage we can endure, for lo, his doom is sure:
One little word shall fell him.[1]

Note

1. Martin Luther, "A Mighty Fortress Is Our God," public domain.

CHAPTER 3

PASSION ALONG THE PATH

It must have been a beautiful spring that year, one in which David was particularly enjoying his reign as king. After all, it had only been a year since he had successfully restored his nation to peace after defeating the Syrians and had also made his army a great military power in the land. Ah, yes! How good the days were!

The rainy season of winter was behind, and many crops were now ready for harvesting—a spring tradition in Israel. Spring also meant that the roads were dry, making travel easier for wagons and chariots. Because of these good travel conditions and the plentiful supply of food, spring had become the traditional time to wage war on enemies, and the armies were usually led by their kings.

But this spring was different. David was ready to wage war against the Ammonites, but instead of leading the army himself, he stayed behind in Jerusalem and sent Joab. Because David abandoned his purpose by staying home from the battle, he was outwitted and encountered many needless struggles.

FOUR QUESTIONS

Satan seeks to outwit us, God's people, in ways that will divert us from God's path. By rerouting us, he can embroil us in problems and situations that keep us from God's destiny for our life. As we seek to be the outwitters rather than the outwitted, here are four key questions we should ask ourselves.

1. **Am I prepared for the warfare ahead?** We do not have to make a conscious decision to engage the enemy before we find ourselves in warfare. Our enemy is actively waging a battle against us whether or not we fight back. Nevertheless, a wise Christian will look at the warfare in which he or she is involved and ask if he or she is truly prepared to move forward in the fight.

2. **In what area do I need the most training (i.e. finances, vision, family, etc.)?** As we take stock of our preparedness, we will need to seek out training in any areas of lack in our own lives or in our families that are weak.

3. **What war am I in?** God has not called us to fight every battle. It is important to know our role and

how the Lord is positioning each of us in the war.

4. **Is there an area in my life in which the enemy is outwitting me?** We will devote much of this chapter to looking at this question in some detail. How is it that we are so susceptible to becoming outwitted by the enemy?

> A WISE CHRISTIAN WILL LOOK AT THE WARFARE IN WHICH HE OR SHE IS INVOLVED AND ASK IF HE OR SHE IS TRULY PREPARED TO MOVE FORWARD IN THE FIGHT.

THE TWO TYPES OF PASSION

The first type of passion is a driving or compelling force, a dominating emotion, a strong desire or a potent enthusiasm. This is the type of passion that is commonplace today. But in the *King James Version*, the word "passion" is only used once in the New Testament. It appears in Acts 1:3 to describe a different type of passion. Here the word means the suffering of Christ on the cross—hence the title of Mel Gibson's movie *The Passion of the Christ*. For us, then, this second type of passion is entering into the sufferings and endurance of our Lord against temptation; experiencing His death in our flesh; and receiving and experiencing His resurrection life.

The Greek word used for passion in Acts 1:3 is from the root word *pathos,* which is defined as path. From this we can see that our passion is linked to our path. If the enemy can cause us to become passive as we traverse our God-given path, then our passion for God will become misdirected. Passivity will cause us to quit resisting the enemy who is in our path; the enemy can then outwit us by misdirecting our passions and causing us to fall into sin.

That is exactly what happened to David. At the time when he was supposed to enter into war, he fell into passivity and chose to stay home. Because he stayed home, he was not in the place God wanted him to be and the enemy took advantage of him. There are times when we, like David, are called to war. We war against everything that is set against our destiny or our accomplishing the fullness of our path. If do not go into battle when God calls us to war, then we will be in serious danger of being outwitted by the enemy—he can stir up our passivity into a passion that God never intended. Success means that you're at the right place at the right time, doing the right thing. God blesses that. When we are in this place, God's favor rests upon us and we can see the true, God-given desires and passions of our hearts fulfilled.

Ungodly Passions

David belonged on the battlefield, not looking out on to Bathsheba's roof where she was bathing. As lust for this woman filled his heart, he further entertained temptation by inquiring about her. This demonstrates how our thoughts can be led astray by our emotions. Passion is a powerful, controlling sentiment that can overwhelm our state of mind and influence our actions. If we never bring our emotions under the control of the Holy Spirit, our emotions will tend to become hooked into ungodly passions that lead to sin. As David continued to give place in his mind to his misguided passions, those passions turned into the actions of committing

IF WE DO NOT GO INTO BATTLE WHEN GOD CALLS US TO WAR, THEN WE WILL BE IN SERIOUS DANGER OF BEING OUTWITTED BY THE ENEMY.

adultery with Bathsheba and the murder of her husband, Uriah. Because of David's murderous scheme, many others were killed on that day.

David's passivity caused him to be diverted from his path; his passivity turned into ungodly passion and sin, and he suffered the consequences.

- Murder became a constant threat in his family (see 2 Sam. 13:29-30; 18:14-15; 1 Kings 2:23-24).
- His household rebelled against him (see 2 Sam. 15:13).
- Absalom disgraced David by sleeping with his wives in public view (see 2 Sam. 16:20-23).
- The child he had with Bathsheba died (see 2 Sam. 12:18).[1]

The enemy had outwitted him, and as a result David paid a great price.

There are demonic forces that work to tempt us in whatever way they can, and every time we fall into a particular sin, our passion becomes misdirected in some way. God wants us to be a passionate people. While walking in that passion, we have to stay on the right path.

Misdirected Paths

When our desire deviates from our true purpose, the enemy will give us opportunities to make wrong choices and sin. The enemy is after our will. If he can misdirect our desire, he can eventually capture our will; when he captures our will, we're not accomplishing the purpose of God and will suffer many needless consequences.

A great illustration of this is found in Proverbs 7, in which a young man gives in to the temptations of a seductress. Let's look carefully at the following passage to see how our path can become diverted.

> My son, keep my words, and treasure my commands within you. Keep my commands and live, and my law as the apple of your eye. Bind them on your fingers; write them on the tablet of your heart. Say to wisdom, "You are my sister," and call understanding your nearest kin, that they may keep you from the immoral woman, from the seductress who flatters with her words (Prov. 7:1-5).

In the opening statement of this proverb, God tells us that we need His commandments to take root down deep in our spirits so that when the seductress comes, we won't be drawn away from our path. It is important to note that the "seductress" here is not only a woman, but also represents a seducing spirit that will attempt to divert our passion away from God. That spirit says to us, "Wait a minute. Come here." If we even give her a second look, suddenly, instead of having the strength to resist, we feel a pulling away and a shift in our desire. Before long, instead of our spirit's being in communion with God, our spirit begins to come into communion with another spirit.

> For at the window of my house I looked through my lattice, and saw among the simple, I perceived among the youths, a young man devoid of understanding, passing along the street near her corner; and he took the path to her house (Prov. 7:6-8).

This young man's passion was not for God; instead, his affections put him on the path to the seductress's house, and she continued to entice him.

> Come, let us take our fill of love until morning; let us delight ourselves with love (Prov. 7:18).

The enemy is going to try to convince us that he can bring a delight in us, which is an emotional response. He's going to have to counterfeit the love of God in some way, now that he's moved us off the path of God's love. Often, this illustration is sexual in nature, but it can apply to any fulfillment of ungodly lust. When we aren't being directed by the Holy Spirit, our body will seek to fulfill its senses in ways that cause it to feel good.

> With her enticing speech she caused him to yield, with her flattering lips she seduced him. Immediately he went

after her, as an ox goes to the slaughter, or as a fool to the correction of the stocks, till an arrow struck his liver. As a bird hastens to the snare, he did not know it would cost his life (Prov. 7:21-23).

Here we see that sin will affect us physically. It will affect even the organs of our body once we deviate from the path and align ourselves with the enemy. This is particularly true of sexual sins. This was very clearly illustrated to me once when I was ministering. I got a word of knowledge that a man present at the meeting had had sex with a witch and, as a result, was suffering from disease in his liver. Not wanting to publicly embarrass this suffering man, I said that I would be in my room for two hours that afternoon, and that whoever it was could come for private ministry. That afternoon I heard a knock on the door. When I opened it, there were eight men who had come for deliverance, all having had sex with witches and all suffering from some kind of liver disease! Sin defiles the body often in ways we do not understand.

The English Puritan preacher Richard Sibbes once said, "Satan gives an apple, but he looks to deprive us of a paradise."[2] Oh, how true this is. Therefore whenever the enemy makes us an offer, we should consider not what we would gain but what we would lose.

The Problem with Passivity

One of Satan's most effective ploys is to lure us into passivity. We saw this at the beginning of this chapter when David did not follow his path to war. When we lose our passion and zeal for God and for His purposes in our life, we are then at our most vulnerable for becoming diverted from our path and into ungodly passions.

If the enemy can ever get us into passivity so we are not communing, we end up just wandering through life and in danger of Satan's filling our mind with lies. This is one circumstance he will use to develop strongholds in our mind. Because of passivity, our thoughts are not connected to the mind of Christ, and we

ONE OF SATAN'S MOST EFFECTIVE PLOYS IS TO LURE US INTO PASSIVITY.

cannot see the full plan that God has for us. Think of a room in which stacks and stacks of materials have accumulated. Those stacks have not been dusted in years. It's hard to know what is in the stacks. Cobwebs have overtaken the room. That is what our mind looks like when the devil brings us into passivity. *Shake out those cobwebs! Get them out of your brain.* We periodically need deliverance in our lives, simply because we can so easily fall into places of passivity and end up in a position in which the enemy can start trying to convince us of lies about God and about our God-given destiny.

A RETURN TO PASSION

In order for us to be totally free, we must submit to death. We have to enter into the second type of passion and experience the death of the Cross. To have this kind of passion is to experience His death in our flesh. We must not be afraid of this death—such a fear will prevent us from entering into the Resurrection and crossing over into our next level of power and authority.

Part of this death in our flesh will entail suffering and trials. The truth is that whenever there is warfare in our lives that we will need to press through, there will also be an amount of suffering that we will encounter in overcoming. However, it is through that process that our godly passion originates and is completed. Via this overcoming in the midst of great difficulties, we are able to move into new dimensions of God's best for our lives.

At the time of this writing, my coauthor, Rebecca Sytsema and her husband, Jack, were undergoing a difficult type of suffering in that their oldest son, Nicholas, has autism. This has been a deeply painful and incredibly trying experience, affecting every area of their lives and draining them of resources. Yet as they have walked this situation out over the past several years and have remained faithful to the Lord, He has infused them with a tremendous new passion they could not otherwise have known.

Their hearts burn with a desire to minister to other children and families who are struggling with autism. As a result, the Lord has led them to Florida where Jack is working fulltime in the field of autism. They have also begun their own ministry called Children of Destiny, through which they minister to individuals and families who have been broken through autism. Their ministry reaches literally thousands each and every day, offering God's hope for the future. Could this passion have been birthed without the suffering they have experienced? They would be the first to tell you that the answer is no. Trials are difficult, and the fire can be intense, but godly passion birthed out of times of suffering and endurance has much greater depth and potential for changing the world than passion acquired by any other means.

When we don't sense the life of Christ flowing through us, we need to ask the Lord, *What has happened to my passion? In the midst of my circumstance, Lord, did I just get tired and quit withstanding?* In truth, we can pray until we are green. We can do all sorts of religious activities. But if we don't resist the enemy—the temptation toward passivity and all other temptations—in the midst of that trial and if we do not let that trial bring the working of the Cross into us, then we won't really enter into the passion and fullness of life that the Lord has for each of us. And having God's passion as we walk in wisdom and revelation is the key to protecting ourselves from becoming outwitted by the enemy.

Notes
1. *Life Application Bible* (Wheaton, IL: Tyndale House Publishers, Inc., 1988), p. 477.
2. Richard Sibbes, "The Rich Pearl," *Lamb Lion Net.* http://www.lamb lion.net/Quotations/sibbes.htm (accessed May 20, 2004).

CHAPTER 4

THE MIND-SET OF WAR

Few of us equate God's revelation of peace in worship with a release to go to war. We want peace, but peace at what price? Some think that if we show ourselves to be peace-loving people, we will never have to war. In 1938, France just wanted to live in peace. So they ignored their neighbor Germany, which was preparing for war. But the desire for peace did not bring peace. Germany was able to take possession of France in a very short period of time. It is not our inclination for war that invites war; rather, it is our having possession of something that someone else wants. The enemy has declared war on us. He wants our worship, our loyalty and our souls. He is willing to war for these things. We are at war, whether we want to be or not.

Passivity does not bring peace and never has. History has shown us that as long as we are willing to give up what is ours, we will not have to face war. If we give up our possessions, war can be averted. If we give up our rights, war can be averted. If we give our children as slaves, war can be averted. But wait! How far are we willing to go here? That's a good question for the Church today. We've given up prayer in our schools. We've given up the rights of the unborn. We've allowed a small minority to determine what is acceptable in society, such as same-sex marriages and allowing those couples to adopt children.

We've allowed ourselves to be ridiculed for taking any kind of stand for righteousness. Wendell Phillips, in a speech before the Massachusetts Anti-Slavery Society in 1852, said, "Eternal vigilance is the price for liberty."[1] We haven't been vigilant and much is lost. Now God wants back what is His and He is looking to us to go get it.

> I beseech you therefore, brethren, by the mercies of God, that you present your bodies a living sacrifice, holy, acceptable to God, which is your reasonable service. And do not be conformed to this world, but be transformed by the renewing of your mind, that you may prove what is that good and acceptable and perfect will of God (Rom. 12:1-2).

It is time for a breakout! The word "conformity" means to be formed to a blueprint of the world. The enemy longs to form us according to his blueprint, but God wants to transform our minds to the way that He thinks. Once that occurs, we can gain wisdom from God. Wisdom will dismantle any plan of the enemy and outwit him.

THE IMPORTANCE OF WISDOM

In order to gain the revelation we need to war with the enemy and see him defeated, we need the wisdom of God. The devil is by no means stupid. He is crafty and deceitful and he has been working against God's purposes much longer than any of us has

> ## THE DEVIL HAS BEEN WORKING AGAINST GOD'S PURPOSES MUCH LONGER THAN ANY OF US HAS BEEN WORKING FOR GOD!

been working for God! He knows what he is doing and how to divert us from God's perfect path. In order to overthrow his plans against us, we need access to the wisdom of the Ancient of Days, not only to gain strategy for today but also to see what snares the devil is setting in days ahead. God will release ancient wisdom to us so that we can outwit the devil in our present-day battles. We, therefore, need to constantly seek the Lord for new and fresh wisdom for each new day and each new battle we face.

Proverbs 3:13-26 gives us a great list of the benefits of godly wisdom that should motivate anyone to seek Him for wisdom.

The passage begins like this: "Happy is the person who finds wisdom and gains understanding. For the profit of wisdom is better than silver, and her wages are better than gold. Wisdom is more precious than rubies; nothing you desire can compare with her." The passage goes on to list the following benefits of living in godly wisdom.

- "Wisdom is a tree of life to those who embrace her; happy are those who hold her tightly" (v. 18, NLT). Through concerns of this world and cares that overwhelm us, Satan will often try to thwart the abundant life God has promised to us. But when we have the wisdom of the Lord, we can see our way past the circumstances of the moment and not spiral into defeat. The ongoing strength and energy we need for life and happiness are products of living in the wisdom of God.

- "By wisdom the LORD founded the earth; by understanding he established the heavens. By his knowledge the deep fountains of the earth burst forth, and the clouds poured down rain" (vv. 19-20, NLT). Satan would love for us to forget the majesty and power of the God we serve. The wisdom of the Lord causes us to remember His awesome creative power, not only to form the earth and the heavens but also to supply us with everything we need to sustain our lives. Wisdom will cause us to see our supply for days ahead, even when Satan has hidden it from us.

- "Have two goals: wisdom—that is, knowing and doing right—and common sense. Don't let them slip away, for they fill you with living energy, and are a feather in your cap" (vv. 21-22, TLB). God has a certain stature that He longs to bring to His people. He will establish them in places of honor and respect so that His will can be done on Earth. Wisdom will cause us to walk in the place God intends for us so that His purposes can be accomplished through us.

• "[Wisdom will] keep you safe from defeat and disaster and from stumbling off the trail" (v. 23, *TLB*). Satan has defeat and disaster planned for each of us. Wisdom is an indispensable tool to outwit his schemes.

• "You can lie down without fear and enjoy pleasant dreams. You need not be afraid of disaster or the destruction that comes upon the wicked, for the LORD is your security. He will keep your foot from being caught in a trap" (vv. 24-26, *NLT*). In wisdom we will find great peace. As we walk in the Lord's wisdom, we can rest in Him, knowing that our path is certain and that our footing is secure.

GOD'S SURPRISE FOR THE DEVIL

It is wonderfully true that as we seek the Ancient of Days for wisdom, we will see God surprise the devil. And why should that surprise us? There are many instances in Scripture in which God thwarted Satan's plans through wisdom that Satan did not have access to. The most significant of these occasions was the Cross. Satan was so wrapped up in seeing that Jesus was humiliated, discredited and eliminated from the earth, that he did not see that the Cross was the very instrument God would use to liberate the human race from death, hell and the grave. Satan thought he was gaining a huge victory as the tide of public sentiment turned against Jesus. Even though the Old Testament prophets had predicted what would occur, Satan did not have the ability to see God's wisdom—that through His death, Jesus would establish a path to freedom from Satan's grip over each of us. The Cross completely surprised and defeated the devil.

THE CROSS COMPLETELY SURPRISED AND DEFEATED THE DEVIL.

God can do the same for us. God can use even those things that look like defeat in our lives to establish His victory and authority. He does this by giving us wisdom to which the enemy does not have access.

> However, we speak wisdom among those who are mature, yet not the wisdom of this age, nor of the rulers of this age, who are coming to nothing. But we speak the wisdom of God in a mystery, the hidden wisdom which God ordained before the ages for our glory, which none of the rulers of this age knew; for had they known, they would not have crucified the Lord of glory. But as it is written: "Eye has not seen, nor ear heard, nor have entered into the heart of man the things which God has prepared for those who love Him." But God has revealed them to us through His Spirit. For the Spirit searches all things, yes, the deep things of God (1 Cor. 2:6-10).

This passage reveals the following important keys for surprising the devil through wisdom:

- God has wisdom greater than any worldly wisdom.
- Powers and principalities do not have access to this wisdom.
- The authority of demonic forces is limited.
- There is wisdom that has been hidden since the beginning of time for His glory.
- Through the redemptive cross of Jesus Christ, we have access to this wisdom.
- God is prepared to release this wisdom to us as we get to know Him intimately through prayer.
- This wisdom will overthrow high places and release captives.
- Wisdom dismantles demonic structures and dethrones thrones of iniquity.[2]

HOW TO OBTAIN WISDOM

Proverbs 4 shows us that we are to be seekers of wisdom. In fact, verse 7 in *The Living Bible* declares, "Getting wisdom is the most important thing you can do!"

Intimacy with God

There is no way we can hear the voice of the Lord without drawing near to Him. The primary way of doing this is through worship and prayer. Without making a commitment to seek God in these ways, we will never be able to gain an understanding of His wisdom. It is from a place of intimacy that we can tap into all of

God's covenant promises to us. But as with any covenant, if we don't hold up our end of the deal, we will not reap the full benefits of the covenant. If we don't seek true and intimate relationship with God, we, like Satan, will not have access to His wisdom and strategy for moving forward, because we will not be positioned to hear His voice when He speaks to us.

Meditation on God's Word

For 30 days they had wept and mourned the death of their great leader—the one who had led them out of centuries of terrible slavery. They had followed him faithfully for 40 years as they maneuvered the wilderness in search of God's Promised Land. Most of a generation had died, and now Moses was gone.

In his place rose Joshua, whose job it was to take possession of the land God had prepared for the Israelites. Joshua had received great promises from God. Every place the sole of his foot touched, God would give to Israel. None of his enemies would be able to stand up against him. God would never leave or forsake him. But in order for Joshua to gain the wisdom he needed to possess the land, God instructed him to meditate. Joshua 1:8 says, "Do not let this Book of the Law depart from your mouth; meditate on it day and night, so that you may be careful to do everything written in it. Then you will be prosperous and successful" (*NIV*).

Why was meditation such a key to Joshua's success? Among other things, it was in his times of meditation that the Lord spoke to Joshua His strategy for moving forward. The strategy for conquering a particular enemy would not work against another. Joshua needed a fresh, new revelation for every step he took. To understand the strategy he needed for the next move, he had to connect with God. And he did so through prayer and meditation.

If we will willingly take time to meditate on God's Word, He will bring success to our lives. Why is that? The Bible contains great wisdom and strategy for our lives that transcend time. But if we just read the Bible without taking the time to give it

IF WE WILL WILLINGLY TAKE TIME TO MEDITATE ON GOD'S WORD, HE WILL BRING SUCCESS TO OUR LIVES.

thought, we don't have the opportunity to really understand what we've just read. Without meditation, how can the words of truth provide refreshment to our soul and spirit? How can we understand the true wisdom lying beneath the words? And how can prayer flow out of a passage that has been read but not understood?

Pastor and author Donald S. Whitney put it this way: "Meditation is the missing link between Bible intake and prayer. . . . There should be a smooth, almost unnoticeable transition between Scripture input and prayer output so that we move even closer to God in those moments. This happens when there is the link of meditation in between."[3]

Sin and Iniquity Overthrown

Sin and iniquity in our lives will keep us separated from God in a way that we will be unable to hear His voice. Satan's objective is to block the plans of God by gaining legal access to us through sin. From that position, he is then able to derail us. We need to understand the full impact of sin on our lives, especially those secret or besetting sins that we may be reluctant to fully vanquish. Sin is a powerful roadblock that keeps us from outwitting the devil. Few of the principles outlined in this book will have much of an affect unless we have dealt with our sin. But here, again, God will provide wisdom and insight to those who genuinely seek Him to overthrow sin in their lives.

Affections Guarded

After admonishing us to seek wisdom, Proverbs 4 goes on to declare, "Above all else, guard your affections. For they influence everything else in your life" (v. 23, *TLB*). This principle cannot be stated any better. As human beings, our affections (those things that we love or have a special attachment to) are linked with our desires. The word "affection" is defined as the emotional realm of love, a feeling, devotion or sentiment; a bent or disposition of mind able to sway reason. If the fire of God is not in our affections, we often lack the faith we need to move forward in God's plan for our lives. If an affection has gained a hook in our hearts, it will have a hook in our lives because it will be able to sway our reason. If we have not guarded our affections and brought them under the Lordship of Christ, our reasoning will, therefore, not be able to accept the wisdom of God.

The Power of Lies Broken

Every lie we receive in our minds works like an anesthetic to deaden us. In the Bible this is described as a spirit of slumber. It attaches itself to an unbelieving, mocking, blasphemous spirit so that we can't capture the truth and be liberated. At a particular time, it'll make us go to sleep to prevent us from hearing truth. The enemy will whisper false arguments and philosophy to exalt himself above the knowledge of God in our minds. So we are to cast down these things.

We have another dynamic in that sinful acts are iniquitous. Iniquity forms a pattern and a deviation from God's plan in a bloodline. Once that iniquity is there, it is passed on to the next generation. If we don't guard our hearts (according to Prov. 4:23), that iniquity becomes part of the DNA structure that we pass on to our children.

God-Given Authority Heeded

One of my favorite stories is found in Matthew 8:5-13—the story of the centurion. This man goes to Capernaum to find Jesus to plead with Him to heal his servant, who is dreadfully tormented and paralyzed. Because of this man's cry for help, Jesus said,

> "I will come and heal him." The centurion answered and said, "Lord, I am not worthy that You should come under my roof. But only speak a word, and my servant will be healed. For I also am a man under authority, having soldiers under me. And I say to this one, 'Go,' and he goes; and to another, 'Come,' and he comes; and to my servant, 'Do this,' and he does it" (vv. 7-9).

Jesus marveled at this man's faith. In fact, He called it great faith and exclaimed that He had not seen this type of faith in all of Israel (see v. 10). He then said to the centurion, "Go your way; and as you have believed, so let it be done for you" (v. 13). The centurion's "servant was healed that same hour" (v. 13).

> One of the greatest lessons of faith is the relationship
> between faith and authority. My father died premature-
> ly when I was 16. Even though I lived through some trau-
> matic times, I was never left fatherless. God placed
> fathers and mothers in my life so that I would never be
> outside an authority structure. I believe this has been a
> key to my personal development of faith. . . . The
> understanding of authority is a key to unlock our des-
> tiny and enter into God's promises by faith.[4]

We must recognize the voice of authority in our lives, particularly the voice of the Holy Spirit, so that we can advance in the
promises the Lord has for us.

The Human Spirit Filled with the Holy Spirit

The Holy Spirit inhabits our human spirit and connects us to
the heavenly abiding place that God has prepared for us. It is in
this abiding place that the Lord will reveal His wisdom to us.
The Holy Spirit is also the One who reveals God's will to us and
empowers us to accomplish it. He is our helper. Thus, when we
cry out for help, we are crying out for a manifestation of His
presence—and in His presence, we will gain the wisdom and
understanding needed to overthrow the enemy in our lives.

WISDOM AND DISCERNMENT LINKED

When God speaks His wisdom to us, it is often through our spiritual intuition, known as discernment. Through our spiritual

discernment, God communicates to our spirits when something is not right or when the enemy has linked himself to a particular situation or place. "Discernment" is the act of distinguishing, recognizing, discriminating or perceiving by sight or other sense.

WHEN GOD SPEAKS HIS WISDOM TO US, IT IS OFTEN THROUGH OUR SPIRITUAL INTUITION, KNOWN AS DISCERNMENT.

God can use our senses to help us discern our spiritual surroundings. For example, the Bible speaks of the fragrance of His knowledge, or the fragrance of Christ (see 2 Cor. 2:14-15). This can be an actual fragrance that we can perceive with our sense of smell. People who discern in this way regularly report that they know when demonic forces are lingering because the forces have a particularly foul odor about them.

Throughout the Bible we read verses in which the Lord asks, "What do you see?" One such instance is recorded in Jeremiah 1:11. When the Lord asked Jeremiah what he saw, he replied, "I see a branch of an almond tree." Verse 12 shows the result: "Then the LORD said to me, 'You have seen well, for I am ready to perform My word.'" The almond was the first tree to bloom. It was also used as a breeding device to increase Jacob's herds. It was one of the best fruits of the land and was given as a gift. Aaron's rod produced ripe almonds, signifying the priesthood to come. The early-appearing white bloom of the almond is linked to the graying head that signifies wisdom. Jeremiah was called to watch and when he saw the almond it meant that spring was coming. When the Lord asked Jeremiah what he saw, the almond branch that he saw with his physical eyes became a spiritual indicator of what was to come.

Starting in verse 13 we read, "And the word of the LORD came to me the second time, saying, 'What do you see?' And I said, 'I see a boiling pot, and it is facing away from the north.' Then the LORD said to me: 'Out of the north calamity shall break forth on all the inhabitants of the land. For behold, I am calling all the families of the kingdoms of the north,' says the LORD" (vv. 13-15). Here again God was using one of Jeremiah's physical senses to bring spiritual insight and wisdom over what was going to occur.

The Lord can use any of our senses to communicate with us. Biblically some examples of this include "taste and see that the Lord is good" (Ps. 34:8), hear the sound calling us to war (see Josh. 6:5; 2 Sam. 5:24) and touch His garment to be made well (see Matt. 9:21). The use of our senses to discern also includes what might be described as intuitive sensing, or what some might call a sixth sense, which is when we know something within our spirit.

Hebrews 5:14 reads, "But solid food belongs to those who are of full age, that is, those who by reason of use have their senses exercised to discern both good and evil." As we spend time communing with God and maturing in Him, we will find that He will use even our senses to provide us with wisdom to outwit our enemy. According to this passage, wisdom comes through the use and exercise of our senses. Therefore, we should ask the Lord to help us discern His wisdom in all things, and to be open to seeing, hearing, tasting, smelling and touching Him in new ways.

We have used the first four chapters of this book to lay the groundwork for understanding both our authority and what we need to be successful in our warfare against Satan. Now let's look at the various types of prayers that, when prayed through the leading and wisdom of the Holy Spirit, will truly outwit the enemy.

Notes

1. Wendell Phillips, quoted in *The Home Book of Quotations*, *9th ed.*, Burton Stevenson, ed., (New York: Dodd Mead, 1964), p. 1106. Quote also attributed to Patrick Henry and Thomas Jefferson, although the Jefferson Library at Monticello classifies the attribution to Jefferson as "spurious." See http://www.monticello.org/library/famquote.html (accessed May 21, 2004).
2. Chuck D. Pierce and Rebecca Wagner Sytsema, *Future War of the Church* (Ventura, CA: Renew, 2001), p. 123.
3. Donald S. Whitney, *Spiritual Disciplines for the Christian Life* (Colorado Springs, CO: Navpress, 1991), p. 67.
4. Chuck D. Pierce and Robert Heidler, *Restoring Your Shield of Faith* (Ventura, CA: Regal Books, 2002), p. 123.

CHAPTER 5

CONFRONTATION, BREAKTHROUGH AND REARGUARD PRAYERS

Many years ago I often found myself staying up late and spending time with the Lord. One night His presence was very strong. While praying, the Lord began to speak to me about the enemy. I was praying for several people, our church, the city in which we lived and for my wife, Pam, who had already gone to bed. This was before we had any children. We had been talking about what to do about the results of medical tests that she had completed that diagnosed her as having a severe case of endometriosis. She had also been diagnosed as barren with a low possibility of ever conceiving. She went to bed with her emotions on a roller coaster.

As I questioned the Lord about this, He spoke a simple word to me: "You can turn the enemy into his own fire!" I knew He was saying that the enemy's plan of destruction could be turned back on him. I began to pray accordingly, not only for Pam but also for all the other burdens that were on my heart. That prayer time was one of the most incredible I have ever experienced because I was both praying and warring. I would worship and then I would war. It was 2 A.M. when I finally went to bed.

I was awakened about an hour later by a visible evil presence standing next to my bed. I said: "In the name of Jesus, who are you?" This presence identified itself as Ashtoreth. It looked like a woman but had a man's voice. The voice from the presence said: "I have come to take your children!" I commanded it to leave in the name of Jesus and by His blood. By this time, Pam was awake. She could also feel the evil in the room.

When the presence left, light filled the room. Pam and I stood and began to shout and worship. The Lord then filled us with faith instead of fear. We had been told that we could not have children. This demon force was telling us that it had come to take our children. The attempt to intimidate us had not worked. Instead, the enemy had overplayed his hand and we came into great faith that the Lord would break barrenness in our lives. It was a strategic revelation in our lives that moved us forward.

THE CONFRONTATION PRAYER

Once we have received strategic revelation from the Lord, we must then obey Him in what He is asking us to do, which includes warfare. There are times when God calls us to confront the powers of darkness at different levels. To confront is to face with hostility or defiance, or to come with opposition. The

ONCE WE HAVE RECEIVED STRATEGIC REVELATION FROM THE LORD, WE MUST THEN OBEY HIM IN WHAT HE IS ASKING US TO DO.

prayer of confrontation directly addresses a structure that has been set in place in opposition to God's will. The prayer of confrontation has become known in missiological terms as a power encounter. C. Peter Wagner defines a power encounter as "a visible, practical demonstration that Jesus Christ is more powerful than the spirits, powers or false gods worshiped or feared by the members of a given people group."[1]

This type of prayer not only outwits the devil but also humiliates him and decreases his level of power in the process. When Jesus was crucified, we saw a clear example of how this works. Referring to that terrible, yet awesome day, Colossians 2:15 reads, "Having disarmed principalities and powers, He made a public spectacle of them, triumphing over them in it."

God allows us to enter into this type of power encounter to show His power over territorial spirits to which a particular group of people has been in bondage. As God displays that His power is greater than that of a demonic structure, that structure begins to crumble and those who have been held captive by fear are then free to follow Christ. In his book *Confronting the Queen of Heaven*, C. Peter Wagner writes a great exhortation on confrontation.

> What level of spiritual warfare does Paul have in mind as he writes to the Ephesians? He says that Jesus is on the right hand of God and "far above all principality and power and might and dominion" (Eph. 1:21). Undoubtedly, Diana of the Ephesians and the daily sacrifices in her ornate temple are in Paul's mind. Jesus is superior to Diana and to all similar territorial spirits, no matter how long they have ruled people groups or cities. The armies of God are being called forth to enforce the rightful rule of the King of kings and Lord of lords on the highest spiritual levels!
>
> There are at least three very important things that the head [Jesus] is telling the body about spiritual warfare:
>
> 1. **Stand against the wiles of the devil.** Paul tells the Ephesians to put on the whole armor of God "that you may be able to stand against the wiles of the devil" (Eph. 6:13). This is not a benign command. It is not something which is easy to do. The reason for this is that the devil is an awesome being. Paul, in the same epistle, calls him "the

prince of the power of the air" (Eph. 2:2). It is hard for me to understand why some Christian leaders insist on trivializing Satan's power. Referring to him as a wimp or as a toothless lion only serves to embolden people to think they can get away with attacking the devil with a fly swatter. I suspect that by saying things like this, some well-intentioned believers are comparing the power of the devil to the power of God, and it is true that there is no contest between the two of them. But this is not the scenario at hand. We are not spectators watching a fight between God and demons. We are the ones whom God has designated to stand against the wiles of the devil. The head tells the body to do it, and, clearly, the head is not going to do it for us.

2. **Engage in proactive spiritual warfare.** In the letter to Ephesus Jesus says, "To him who overcomes, I will give to eat from the tree of life which is in the midst of the Paradise of God" (Rev. 2:7). The word "overcome," which Jesus repeats seven times, is *nikao* in the original Greek. It is a military word meaning "to conquer," in secular Greek, but, according to *The New International Dictionary of New Testament Theology:* "In the New Testament [*nikao*] almost always presupposes the conflict between God and opposing demonic powers" (Vol. 1, p. 650). In other words, it means to do spiritual warfare.

3. **Declare God's wisdom to the principalities.** Paul expresses to the Ephesians his burning desire that "the manifold wisdom of God might be made known by the church to the principalities and powers in the heavenly places" (Eph. 3:10). This is another one of the commands from the head of the body, and it explicitly says that *the church* should make this declaration to the powers in the invisible world. There are many interpretations as to what exactly this might mean, but one of them would be that we declare the gospel of the kingdom of God. The church, by deed and also by word, should remind the territorial spirits over places like Ephesus that the kingdom of God has invaded the kingdom of darkness beginning with the life, death, and resurrection of Jesus Christ. And that the god of this age will no longer blind the minds of unbelievers to the glorious gospel of Christ in Ephesus, Turkey, Japan, Nepal, Calcutta, or in any other place. This kind of a declaration of war will predictably spark negative reactions and counterattacks from the forces of evil and the spiritual battle will be engaged. One of the major apostles of the extraordinary Argentine Revival, now in its seventeenth year, is evangelist Carlos Annacondia. In virtually every one of his meetings, he literally declares the wisdom of God to the devil and to any spiritual principalities that might be in the vicinity. Many times I have

heard him do this in a very loud voice and
with powerful anointing of the Holy Spirit.
The title of his excellent book is: *Listen to Me,
Satan!* (Creation House). When this war cry
goes forth, night after night, things begin to
happen. Demons manifest and are summari-
ly dispatched, sick people are healed mi-
raculously, and sinners literally run to the
platform to get saved. More than two million
have been born again in his campaigns so
far.[2]

Of course, C. Peter Wagner is referring to strategic-level
power encounters with demonic structures dealing with whole
people groups or territories. There are examples of this throughout the Old Testament and the New Testament involving people
such as Moses, David, Elijah, Jesus and Paul. God's heart re-
mains the same today. We need to enter into a mentality that
God will display His power greatly over Earth and over demonic
structures in order to see great throngs loosed from Satan's grip,
and from that mentality pray the prayers of confrontation
according to His will. There are times when God will also call us
into a confrontational type of warfare over demonic structures
on a personal or family level, in which case the three points that
we quoted above also apply.

THE BREAKTHROUGH PRAYER

Have you ever felt stuck in life? Stuck in a narrow place from
which you just couldn't get to the next place God had for you?
You might have been mired in illness, debt, grief, a job situation,

an unhealthy relationship, loss of faith in God or any number of other things; almost everyone has felt frustrated by not being able to break through a situation he or she has faced. Breaking through many life situations can often be a long process that may test our ability to persevere and to believe that God will get us to a new place. We may also feel as though the devil has out-witted us, instead of vice versa.

In her book *The Breaker Anointing*, Barbara Yoder wrote,

God has a great deal for us to possess, but it will take great faith and perseverance. God is continually putting new conquests before us to develop our faith and perse-verance at a higher level. We can decide we want to quit at some point because the gate seems too hard or too unconquerable. We may be tired and weary of the battle. We want to sit down, take a rest, and check out. We have the option of sitting down and living a life of ease. But by doing so we will never reach our potential because fear or weariness overtook us at the threshold. Some make this decision and fail to reach their destiny.

Paul said that he kept pressing on to attain that which he was intended to attain (see Phil. 3:12-14). God apprehended Paul not just to convert him but also to use Paul to accomplish a great ministry, to take the gospel to the Gentiles in many nations. Paul pressed through despite many trials.[3]

The enemy will often get us in a vicious cycle through adverse circumstances. Satan attempts to weaken our faith, dis-illusion us and keep us going around Mount Sinai until we are so weary that we may even forget that there is a Promised Land. We can even see such desperation come over a territory that

Satan has held captive. We must use the power of breakthrough prayer to smash the vicious cycle of unbelief and declare a breaking in the enemy's scheme.

SATAN ATTEMPTS TO KEEP US GOING AROUND MOUNT SINAI UNTIL WE ARE SO WEARY THAT WE MAY FORGET THAT THERE IS A PROMISED LAND.

To break means to cause to come apart by force, to separate into pieces by shattering, to burst and force a way through resulting in splitting a barrier, and to interrupt and bring about suspension of an operation. It is a term that means an offensive thrust that penetrates and carries beyond a defensive line in warfare, a sudden advance in knowledge or technique, a moving through an obstruction, and a disrupting of the continuity or flow of an old system. There are times when God calls us to use prayer to break the power of the enemy.

One of the names and characteristics of God is the Breaker.

The Breaker [the Messiah] will go before them. They will breakthrough, pass in through the gate and go out through it, and their King will pass on before them, the Lord at their head (Mic. 2:13, *Amp.*).

The Lord is ready to establish Himself at the gates of our lives, families, relationships, churches, cities and nations. Here are some of the principles and accompanying results of breakthrough power:

1. **Our light will break forth (see Isa. 58:8).** Light dispels the darkness. Therefore, in order for our light to break through, we need to ask Him to remove any darkness within us. As our light breaks forth, we are able to break through into a new place. Two excellent principles for breaking out of darkness into light include fasting and giving. We should ask the Lord if there is a particular fast He has called us to in order to break out of darkness. Also, if we are willing to give in places in which we have not been willing to give before, we may be surprised at how the Lord will break open new avenues of supply.

2. **Our healing will spring forth (see Isa. 58:8).** The Lord is bringing His Body from grief to glory. Infirmities that have afflicted us for years will flee. We must declare that hidden places of grief will be exposed in us so that we will be made whole. Like Hannah (see 1 Sam. 1), we need to ask the Lord to look upon our afflictions and barrenness, and to make us fruitful.

3. **The new song will break forth (see Isa. 52:9).** Many times when breakthrough occurred in the Word of God the people would sing and rejoice. Moses and Miriam sang when they crossed out of Egypt. Deborah sang when God defeated the Midianites. When we break through, we should rejoice in song and fill the air with praises to God.

4. **A renewed joy will arise in our spirit.** "Do not sorrow, for the joy of the Lord is your strength" (Neh. 8:10). This is a great account of how God's people came to an understanding of their covenant blessings. Nehemiah then told the people not to grieve over what they had missed but break into joy instead. The moment we break through and understand the truth that has been hidden from us, a new joy and hope arise.

5. **New joy causes waste places to be rebuilt.** The breaker anointing causes comfort to be loosed (see Isa. 52:9). That comfort restores what has been desolate and barren and causes places that have laid in ruins to be rebuilt.

6. **New strength will arise in our spirit.** "But those who wait on the LORD shall renew their strength; they shall mount up [breakthrough] with wings like eagles" (Isa. 40:31). We will be able to gain the strength we need to overcome the mountain in our path.

As we are looking at prayers that outwit the devil, we need to allow God to break through for us in a new way. It is time for the Lord to break through, for the Church to break out and for the devil's strategies to break up!

Let God Read Your List

So many times when the enemy comes against us and we need breakthrough, we try to get everyone around us to listen to our problems. However, we should really present our case to the Lord. In 2 Kings 18 and 2 Kings 19, we find that Sennacherib, a type of enemy against God's covenant, was overtaking everyone in his path. This ruler then threatened to defeat Hezekiah and the city of Jerusalem. When Hezekiah faced the most trying time of his life, he inquired of the Lord.

Many times the enemy will draw our eyes to what he is doing and will then convince us that we are next in line. As Hezekiah received a threatening letter from Sennacherib, he presented this letter to the Lord as a prophetic act. We should write down the enemy's threat against us and hold it up to the Lord. This produces an order in our thinking, gives us strategy and paves the way for the Lord Himself to send help to break through and overtake our enemy.

> ## IN ORDER TO SECURE OUR VICTORY AND OUTWIT THE DEVIL IN HIS ATTEMPTS AT BACKLASH, WE NEED TO ALLOW GOD'S STANDARD TO RISE BEHIND US IN REARGUARD PRAYER.

THE REARGUARD PRAYER

Once we see breakthrough in a particular area, it is important for us to understand that the enemy may very well pursue us into our new place with a strategy of backlash against us. In order to secure our victory and outwit the devil in his attempts at backlash, we need to allow God's standard to rise behind us in rearguard prayer. This is a tremendous prayer strategy that I believe the Lord is teaching His people at this time.

> Then your light shall break forth like the morning, your healing shall spring forth speedily, and your righteousness shall go before you; the Glory of the Lord shall be your rear guard (Isa. 58:8).

A rearguard is a detachment of troops detailed to guard the rear of a moving column. The rearguard is generally used for security during a forward movement, but it is also a detachment concerned with delaying the pursuit of a main military body in retreat. In *The Art of War*, Sun Tzu wrote, "Ground that is of great advantage to either side is contentious ground. . . . On contentious ground, hurry up your rearguard."[4] We live in contentious times and the ground that the Body of Christ has taken is very important.

James Robison wrote,

> In our spiritual struggle, we must show the same resolve as we have shown in the war on terrorism. But we must rely on the promises and power of God, rather than on the might of our armed forces. When the enemy raves and rants, we must remember that more than 60 times in the Old and New Testaments, God tells us to "fear not." In many other verses, like the one above, He assures us of His protection against anything Satan can deploy against us. He will drive out the enemy before us (Deut. 18:12). He will be our rearguard (Isa. 58:8).[5]

Remember Isaiah 52:12: "The LORD will go before you, and

the God of Israel will be your rearguard." God promises not only to look out for us as we go into battle, but also to be our rearguard after the battle. Nevertheless, we need to bear in mind that when God has worked mightily, when God has used us significantly, when there has been great spiritual breakthrough, we cannot allow ourselves to be spiritually careless. After a successful battle, we must give ourselves that all-important order: "Shields up!"

The life of David is one of the best examples of rearguard praying. Once David had a breakthrough over the Philistines, God had to secure his victory, because David's enemy mounted up another attack against him. That is what I see happening in our lives and in our nation. The enemy has a strategy of backlash against us.

We must pray from God's covenant plan of protection. God had a covenant with David. When I pray for individuals or regions, and especially our nation, I approach it from the standpoint of covenant. Psalm 89:3-4 reads,

> I have made a covenant with My chosen, I have sworn to My servant David: "Your seed I will establish forever, and build up your throne to all generations."

Verses 20-23 show how our covenant with God positions us to outwit the schemes of our enemy:

> I have found My servant David; with My holy oil I have anointed him, with whom My hand shall be established; also My arm shall strengthen him. The enemy shall not outwit him, nor the son of wickedness afflict him. I will beat down his foes before his face, and plague those who hate him.

In the appendix of this book, we present a 32-day prayer guide that is helpful in securing our victory through rearguard praying.

Notes

1. C. Peter Wagner, *Confronting the Powers* (Ventura, CA: Regal Books, 1996), p. 102.
2. C. Peter Wagner, *Confronting the Queen of Heaven* (Colorado Springs, CO: Wagner Publications, 2001), pp. 31-35.
3. Barbara Yoder, *The Breaker Anointing* (Colorado Springs, CO: Wagner Publications, 2001), p. 43.
4. Sun Tzu, *The Art of War* (n.p.: n.d.), n.p.
5. Source unknown.

CHAPTER 6

THE PRAYER OF TRAVAIL AND AGONY

We learn from Psalm 127:3 that "children are a heritage from the Lord, [and] the fruit of the womb is a reward." The Psalm goes on: "Happy is the man who has his quiver full of them; they shall not be ashamed, but shall speak with their enemies in the gate" (v. 5). There is a desperate, agonizing pain of the soul that comes with barrenness.

My wife, Pam, and I understand the agony of barrenness as it was ten years into our marriage before we were able to have children. There were times of desperation during those years and times we agonized before the Lord. But God heard the desperate cries of our heart for children and brought a miraculous healing to Pam's body that allowed her to conceive. Since that time she has become familiar with the travailing pain of birth, having given birth to six children.

WE AGONIZE WHEN SOMETHING GOD INTENDS TO BE HAS NOT YET MANIFESTED, AND WE TRAVAIL AS WE BIRTH GOD'S NEW THING.

Because what we experience in the natural often mirrors what we experience in the spiritual, we can see that there are times when agony and travail are appropriate precursors and responses to spiritual birth, just as they are to natural birth. We agonize when something God intends to be has not yet manifested, and we travail as we birth God's new thing.

HANNAH'S AGONY

One of the most poignant biblical stories of agonizing before God is the story of Hannah. Israel was in its lowest moral condition as a nation, and the priesthood had fallen into total disarray. However, individuals kept coming to Shiloh to offer sacrifices and to worship the Lord. As required by the Law, Elkahan took his entire family to Shiloh to offer sacrifices.

Hannah, one of Elkahan's two wives, was barren and unfulfilled. She was a desperate woman because she knew that the destiny of her creation had not been fulfilled. This lack of fulfillment had led her into grief and affliction of spirit, which the Bible calls "bitterness of soul." In 1 Samuel 1:10-18, we see how Hannah agonized before the Lord to give her a child. Her agonizing gives us a great pattern to follow. Hannah . . .

- prayed to the Lord.
- wept in anguish (travailed).
- lifted her affliction to the Lord.
- said, "Remember me." In other words, "Remember why I was created."
- pleaded, "Fulfill my request and You can have my first fruit offering."
- told the priest her problem and expressed her emotion.
- asked for favor to come upon her.
- got up in victory.
- birthed the new thing in Israel.

Through her prayer of agony to the Lord, Hannah conceived and gave birth to Samuel. She then fulfilled her vow to the Lord by giving this child to the priest. This act changed the course of Israel. Samuel began to prophesy and the nation began to shift, although not everything went well. As the story progresses, we see that Israel is defeated in war and, as a result, loses the Ark of the Covenant, which represents God's presence among them. This defeat, however, sets the nation of Israel on course to restore the presence of God in the land, which David does many years later when he returns the Ark to its resting place in Jerusalem.

TRAVAILING THAT PRODUCES BIRTH

Be in pain, and labor to bring forth, O daughter of Zion,
like a woman in birth pangs. For now you shall go forth
from the city, you shall dwell in the field, and to Babylon
you shall go. There you shall be delivered; there the
LORD will redeem you from the hand of your enemies
(Mic. 4:10).

A "travail" is defined as a painfully difficult or burdensome
work, particularly the anguish or suffering associated with the
labor of childbirth. What does this have to do with prayer? If we
stop to consider the story of Hannah, we realize that when she
approached the Lord, she was in anguish over her circumstances.
Her plea to God came from the very depths of her being. Her
agony before the Lord did not come purely from the emotion of
an unmet need or desire in her life. It rose up out of her spirit
because, as we previously noted, the destiny for which she had
been created had gone unfulfilled. At the time, she did not know
in the natural that she had been chosen to give birth to Samuel,
a great prophet and judge of Israel. But she knew that she could
not settle for barrenness. She knew that such a condition was
not God's plan for her life.

Before Hannah gave physical birth to Samuel, she travailed for
and birthed something spiritually that overcame the curse of barrenness, not only in her own body, but ultimately in the nation of
Israel through Samuel. When we travail in prayer, what we are
doing is allowing the Holy Spirit to birth something through us.
In her book *Possessing the Gates of the Enemy*, Cindy Jacobs wrote,

There are times when we are called by God to pray strong
prayer and help to birth the will of God into [an] area.

Usually there is a sense of wonder after the prayer, and a sense that God has done something through it. Here are four points to help you recognize the work of the Holy Spirit:

1. Travail is given by God and is not something we can make happen. Travail is often a deep groaning inside, which may be audible or which cannot be uttered, as described in Romans 8:26. . .

2. Travail sometimes comes as a result of praying in an area that others have prayed about before you. God then chooses you to be one of the last pray-ers before the matter is accomplished. You are the one who gives birth to the answer.

3. Those with the gift of intercession will often pray more travailing prayers than those [without the gift].

4. The travail may be short or extended. Some prayers will be accomplished quickly and some will be like labor pangs at different times until the birth of the answer comes.[1]

THE POWER OF TRAVAILING

There is tremendous power in travailing prayer because, as Cindy Jacobs noted, it births the will of God onto Earth. This type of prayer always outwits the devil because he is so strongly opposed by the new thing God is producing as a result of travail. We, therefore, need to have an understanding of what God is wanting to birth through us. We, like Hannah, need to be in tune with what God is ready to bring forth in any given hour. That can only be done through intimacy with God and through a willingness to allow Him to use us in travail.

Many times we have so much that God has put into our spirits, but we don't have the strength to bring it to birth. Isaiah 60:1 paints the picture: "Arise, shine; For your light has come! And the glory of the Lord is risen upon you." *The Amplified Bible*

AS WE ALLOW THE SPIRIT OF THE LORD TO ARISE WITHIN US, WE WILL FIND THAT HE GIVES US THE EXPECTATION OF NEW LIFE.

expands this to "ARISE [from the depression and prostration in which circumstances have kept you—rise to a new life]! Shine (be radiant with the glory of the Lord), for your light has come, and the glory of the Lord has risen upon you!" The word "arise" means to stand firm, to come from a lying down position to an upright position. When we begin to arise and allow God's glory to arise through us, we can take our stand against the powers and principalities that have resisted us. As we allow the Spirit of the Lord to arise within us, we will find that He gives us the expectation of new life and the strength to bring that life to birth.

Once we identify which burden God wants us to pray over,

we begin to agonize and feel the urgency of seeing the burden birthed. The burden becomes our own "baby" as God's heart for seeing that thing brought forth begins to press down on our spirits. With the burden comes an oppression, but it's not the oppression of the devil. If our assignment, for instance, is a travail to break an oppression over certain people, we can actually begin to feel the oppression they are under. We must war until the oppression breaks—until, as in natural childbirth, the opening in the second heaven is large enough so that God's will can come forth on Earth.

THE WISDOM OF CAUTION

Because travailing is such an intense and often misunderstood form of prayer, there are some cautions of which we must be aware.

1. **Timing.** We cannot enter into travailing prayer any more than a woman can enter into labor before her time. It is something the Holy Spirit chooses to do in His time and through whomever He chooses, as long as we are open to allowing Him to work through us in this way. If we try to bring something to birth before its season, like a baby born prematurely, it is much more susceptible to destruction and death than that which is born in the right season.
2. **Becoming overwhelmed.** Cindy Jacobs offers sound advice: "Many times travail can be so strong that it seems to overwhelm the intercessor. Those around need to intercede for the one in travail if this happens in a group situation. We need to help bear the

burden in prayer. . . . We also need to bind the enemy from entering into the travail. One word of caution. The Holy Spirit will rule over our emotions in a time of travail. We must be sure that we don't let our emotions run wild. Intercessors need to walk in the fruit of self-control."[2]

3. **Bearing a false burden.** If someone enters travail but does not have God's burden, they will travail with the wind. Isaiah 26:18 warns, "We have been with child, we have been in pain; we have, as it were, brought forth wind; we have not accomplished any deliverance in the earth, nor have the inhabitants of the world fallen." Many well-meaning Christians travail with the wind because they do not understand God's heart in a matter and move forward in presumption. They either do not know what God is doing or have not taken the time with Him to identify with what He is doing. Instead, they go straight into intercession and get lost in it.

4. **Not completing the assignment.** "This day is a day of trouble, and rebuke, and blasphemy; for the children have come to birth, but there is no strength to bring them forth" (2 Kings 19:3). There are instances in which the timing is right and the burden is right, but we have no strength to bring forth the new birth. We must not grow weary in Spirit, but allow God to bring forth the strength we need to complete our travail, much as we noted earlier in this chapter.

5. **Discounting prayer as travailing because there is no physical manifestation.** Dutch Sheets gives us great perspective on this issue: "I don't believe [travailing prayer] is defined by groaning, wailing, weeping

and hard work. Natural travail certainly is, and spiritual travail *can* include these things. I do not believe, however, it *must* include them, and I'm convinced it is not defined by them. In fact, I believe a person can travail while doing the dishes, mowing the lawn, driving a car—anything a person can do and still pray."[3]

ABIGAIL'S PRAYER

In 1 Samuel 25, we find the story of a wonderful woman named Abigail. At the time the events of this story unfolded, Saul was still pursuing David who was in hiding. David moved down to the Desert of Maon where he asked some of his men to request hospitality and supply from a man named Nabal. Nabal was very wealthy, owned property at Carmel and had a wife named Abigail. She was intelligent and beautiful. He was surly, mean and conniving—a perfect representative of the enemy's characteristics.

Nabal rudely refused David's request for supply for his men. Please do not sympathize with Nabal. In the custom of that day, hospitality was offered to any traveler. Nabal was hostile and defied the custom of that day. He could have been fully blessed by giving. David had even offered payment. Moreover, David and his men had been protecting Nabal's workforce.

When David's men returned to David and communicated Nabal's refusal, David said, "Put on your swords" (see 1 Sam. 25:13). However, Nabal's wise wife interceded. Abigail understood the gravity of the situation. Through her quick response and skillful negotiation, she kept David from taking vengeance upon Nabal and his household. I love how she saw the big picture and left plenty of room for the Lord to intervene.

Abigail provided a perfect picture of intercession as travail. She stood in the gap and travailed. Because of her burden, she actually won the war. God judged her husband, Nabal, and she ended up marrying David. She looked beyond the travail process in her present crisis. She saw the big picture, pressed through and changed the course of history.

THE GREATEST EXAMPLE OF TRAVAIL COMES FROM THE AGONY OF JESUS IN GETHSEMANE.

The Garden of Gethsemane

The greatest example of travail comes from the agony of Jesus in Gethsemane. Here I would like to borrow from the excellent explanation of this given by Dutch Sheets in his book *Intercessory Prayer*.

Without any question Christ's redemption of humanity—the work of intercession—began with His travail in the Garden. Isaiah prophesied of Him: "He shall see of the *travail* of His soul and shall be satisfied" (Isa. 53:11, KJV, emphasis added).

In fulfillment of this, Jesus cried out in Gethsemane saying, "My soul is exceedingly sorrowful, even unto death" (Matt. 26:38, KJV). It was in the Garden of Gethsemane that redemption began and the victory of the entire ordeal was won.

We know that redemption was beginning in this travail for a couple of reasons. Luke tells us Jesus began to shed great drops of blood. Jesus was not simply sweating so profusely that it was like a person bleeding. He was literally bleeding through the pores of His skin, a medical condition known as hematidrosis. We must understand that when the blood of Christ began to flow, redemption was beginning, for it is through the shedding of His blood that we have the cleansing from sin (see Heb. 9:22).

We also know that redemption was beginning in the Garden because when Jesus said, "My soul is exceedingly sorrowful even unto death," the word used for death is *thanatos*. This word is often used for death as the result and penalty of sin. This is the death Adam experienced when he fell.[4]

The Result of Agony

Understanding the suffering and love that Christ demonstrated for us in Gethsemane and at the Cross causes us to have a heart for others. This is the ultimate example of agony that overcomes the strongman and unlocks the prison doors that he has held shut. The prayer of agony causes us to identify with the burden that is on God's heart. Agony leads us to identify with situations. This can include personal issues over people, crisis situations, territorial or national dilemmas, or any number of other things.

When travail comes upon us, we should let the Spirit of God lead us. Romans 8:26 reads, "Likewise the Spirit also helps in our weaknesses. For we do not know what we should pray for as we ought, but the Spirit Himself makes intercession for us with groanings which cannot be uttered." He knows ways to pray that we do not.

THE JUBILEE SEASON

A woman, when she is in labor, has sorrow because her hour has come; but as soon as she has given birth to the child, she no longer remembers the anguish, for joy that a human being has been born into the world. Therefore you now have sorrow; but I will see you again and your heart will rejoice, and your joy no one will take from you (John 16:21-22).

We have not been designed to stay in the place of travail, either physically or spiritually. We have been designed to bring forth new birth and then move into the new season of life that birth brings to us. After travail, release comes. God has a jubilee season over every issue. For instance, if the issue for which we have been travailing involves financial needs, when release comes God will give us or whomever we have been travailing for incredible strategies over how to break debt structures and see financial increase and supply begin to flow. This breakthrough usually includes two arenas: First, there is a financial arena in which God will give strategic insight over how to be released from debt and how to increase income for future advancement; second, there is a relationship arena. When we or the one for whom we have been travailing has relationships that are broken, another type of debt exists. God can find supernatural ways to heal those relationships and cause them to flourish.

During a year of jubilee, labor is suspended. The difficult things for which we have travailed in the past—those things that have been so hard and unyielding, and yet in which we have faithfully pressed through—suddenly come forth and we are released from our hard labor. It is then that we enter into a joy and a faith that we didn't have before, and many things start to fall into place as a new order begins to come. As we agonize, travail and labor for those things that God has laid on our hearts, we should remember there is a time when the birth comes and we are able to enter a season of jubilee, partly because our enemy has been outwitted!

Notes

1. Cindy Jacobs, *Possessing the Gates of the Enemy* (Tarrytown, NY: Chosen Books, 1991), pp. 115-116.
2. Ibid., p. 116.
3. Dutch Sheets, *Intercessory Prayer* (Ventura, CA: Regal Books, 1996), p. 113.
4. Ibid., p. 129.

CHAPTER 7

THE PRAYER OF FAITH

One morning a few years back, as I did every day, I was having a cup of coffee. That particular day imprinted on the surface of the mug I chose were these words: "Faith: The substance of things hoped for, the evidence of things not seen." When I tried to take a sip, I lost my grip and the mug fell, breaking the handle. Immediately the Lord said to me, "I want you to learn how to grasp faith and not lose your handle on it." It was a simple yet profound moment that got me to study faith in a new way.

Faith is amazing! How wonderful it is to know that we can hope and trust in a power that can actually produce results in our lives. I hope that this chapter will help us all grasp faith in such a way that we can outwit the enemy.

The biblical definition of faith is found in Hebrews 11:1-6.

Now faith is the substance of things hoped for, the evidence of things not seen. For by it the elders obtained a good testimony. By faith we understand that the worlds were framed by the word of God, so that the things which are seen were not made of things which are visible. By faith Abel offered to God a more excellent sacrifice than Cain, through which he obtained witness that he was righteous, God testifying of his gifts; and through it he being dead still speaks. By faith Enoch was taken away so that he did not see death, "and was not found, because God had taken him"; for before he was taken he had this testimony, that he pleased God. But without faith it is impossible to please Him, for he who comes to God must believe that He is, and that He is a rewarder of those who diligently seek Him.

Faith is that conviction, confidence, trust and belief that we have in an object or person. Everyone has faith to some degree. But what causes our faith as believers to be different is that our object is God Himself. Therefore, our entire mind must operate around His rulership.

Faith is the persuasion given to us by God, that the things we have not yet seen, we will see. Faith is the pause between what God has said He will do, and our seeing Him act upon His word. If God has said something to us and we have not seen it appear, we must ask Him if we heard Him right or ask Him to give us faith to believe that we will see that which He has said.

Having noted that, there are seven issues of faith that are important for us to understand.

1. **Faith is linked with covenant.** In Genesis 15 we see that God promised Abram an heir who would come from his own body, an heir who would link God's covenant to Abram with all future generations. It took faith on Abram's part to see this promise come to pass. Covenant is initiated by God, but we must respond to it with faith.

2. **Faith is linked with our vision and destiny.** Habakkuk 2:2-4 reads, "Write the vision and make it plain on tablets, that he may run who reads it. For the vision is yet for an appointed time; but at the end it will speak, and it will not lie. Though it tarries, wait for it; because it will surely come, it will not tarry. Behold the proud, his soul is not upright in him; but the just shall live by his faith." We cannot move into God's fullness for us without faith. Therefore, if our vision is clouded, we have trouble operating in faith and need God to infuse us with fresh faith.

3. **Faith comes from listening to the God with whom we have relationship.** "So then faith comes by hearing, and hearing by the word of God" (Rom. 10:17). It doesn't have to be a super-spiritual moment. Often God will pick something as simple and ordinary as dropping a cup of coffee and breaking the mug to speak a profound truth to us. As we listen for God's voice, our faith will continually grow.

4. **Faith works from our love.** "For in Christ Jesus neither circumcision nor uncircumcision avails anything, but faith working through love" (Gal. 5:6). If we do not allow God to work love in us, we cannot

have true faith. It doesn't matter what we do. Without love, faith does not work.

5. **Faith is based on our understanding of authority.** If we have a resistant heart toward authority, faith cannot truly manifest. But when we understand authority, we can have great faith. We see this clearly in Matthew 8:9-10 in which the story is told about Jesus' encounter with the centurion who understood authority: "'For I also am a man under authority, having soldiers under me. And I say to this one, 'Go,' and he goes; and to another, 'Come,' and he comes; and to my servant, 'Do this,' and he does it.' When Jesus heard it, He marveled, and said to those who followed, 'Assuredly, I say to you, I have not found such great faith, not even in Israel!' "

6. **Faith is the element of our relationship that must be demonstrated.** James 2:18 reads, "But someone will say, 'You have faith, and I have works.' Show me your faith without your works, and I will show you my faith by my works." We can't live in passivity. If we are not demonstrating our relationship with God, we are not operating in faith. It may be easy to hide in a prayer closet endlessly, but without demonstrating faith to the world, we are not pleasing God. It is something He requires of us.

7. **Faith can be increased.** Luke 17:5 reads, "And the apostles said to the Lord, 'Increase our faith.'" Where we are now in faith doesn't mean that's all we're to have. God gives each one of us a measure of faith, and that measure of faith can be increased.

THE CONTENTION OVER FAITH

Faith is an essential element in outwitting the enemy. In fact, we can't outwit him without faith—and he knows it. Therefore, the enemy will contend with us viciously to weaken our faith. There are some basic strategies he uses to undo our faith: (1) murmuring and complaining, which perpetuate unbelief within us;

FAITH IS AN ESSENTIAL ELEMENT IN OUTWITTING THE ENEMY.

(2) self-pity, which causes us to become self-centered instead of God-centered; and (3) anger and bitterness, which harden our hearts before the Lord so we cannot approach Him in faith.

There are five major strategies that the devil uses to cut off our faith:

1. **Cutting off our vision.** Without a vision, we will be unable to move forward in God's redemptive gifting in our lives and will be stuck in the same place long after God would have moved us on.
2. **Causing us to doubt God's goodness for the present day.** Satan wants to rob us of any joy and faith we have for seeing God's goodness *today*. If he succeeds, discouragement will overtake us.
3. **Deepening the root of unbelief.** This is where mur-

muring comes into the picture. Murmuring waters unbelief and allows its roots to grow within us. From those roots, we speak words of unbelief and can defile everything around us.

4. **Inviting greater adversity into our life.** Not all the warfare we experience is because God intended that we fight this or that battle. When we get off track in our faith, we can find ourselves walking right into the enemy's encampment and having to fight our way out of a place we were never supposed to visit.

5. **Causing us to release cursing rather than blessing.** When we fall out of faith, it is easy to lose sight of God's good gifts around us and to see all the negative circumstances instead. When we allow negativity to flow out of us, we enter into cursing instead of blessing that which is around us.

From the effects of these strategies, we can easily see why the enemy seeks to engage us in a battle for our faith. Furthermore, the enemy knows that, without faith, we cannot please God. We can pray all day long, but if we do not pray in faith, we really do not touch God's heart. I remember when the Lord spoke to me and said, *Above all, take up the shield of faith that quenches all the fiery darts of the enemy.* This statement was pretty clear—if I could get my shield of faith in place then I could outwit the enemy.

THE PRAYER OF FAITH

The prayer of faith is the gift of faith the Holy Spirit gives us that activates and permeates our entire being, aligning us with the will of God as we agree with Him. When we voice this faith or make a decree of God's will on Earth, we see things happen. In this type of prayer, we fully agree with God and His purposes on Earth. Even a herd of wild horses and every legion of demons cannot move us from our alignment with God's plan.

The prayer of faith saves, heals, forgives and liberates. The prayer of faith is fervent, earnest and filled with energy. The prayer of faith goes beyond our passions and emotions. As we pray in faith, the Holy Spirit begins to pave the way for a miracle to occur in our natural environment. Elijah demonstrated this principle for us. Even though he had emotions just as we do, he prayed the prayer of faith and miracles followed. Elisha entered into this type of praying and received a double-portion anointing of the faith and miracles Elijah had displayed.

GOOD GRADES

Many years ago, Pam and I were the administrators of a children's home. I was there as executive director, and she was there to be my wife and support. One night, the houseparents of the cottage of older boys unexpectedly left the home for personal reasons. We had no choice but to take on this cottage of eight wild boys ourselves.

Joseph was staying in the cottage. He was a 13-year-old Hispanic boy whose mother had been imprisoned; he did not know his natural father. Joseph had seen and experienced more than many adults do in a lifetime. When it came time for Pam and I to leave the children's home, we took Joseph with us and adopted him. I can't say it was easy to raise him because his past still had a grip that was holding his future captive. However, he was a precious kid, my wife loved him, God loved him, and I had been chosen to father him.

In Joseph's senior year of high school, I was at my wit's end and finally decided to send him back from whence he came. One day I left work early and came home from my office to tell Pam of my decision. When I walked through the door, she said to me,

THE PRAYER OF FAITH SAVES, HEALS, FORGIVES AND LIBERATES. THE PRAYER OF FAITH IS FERVENT, EARNEST AND FILLED WITH ENERGY.

"I was praying for Joseph today and the Lord told me that He was going to fill him with the Holy Spirit." She had been praying and was filled with faith. I thought, *Oh, great.* I was not filled with faith, and I knew the war would continue. But I also knew he needed to stay.

The only thing the Lord had ever spoken to me about Joseph was one sentence: *He is called to be an A and B student.* This was hard to grasp by faith since by sight I never saw As and Bs on his report cards. He did manage to make Cs since he needed that grade level to continue playing sports. He attended college after graduation and again, only made Cs. Next he enlisted in the Air Force. He married and has four beautiful children and a wife who graduated from college magna cum laude.

Sometimes it takes time to see a word manifest. When Joseph and his family were visiting one Christmas Eve 20 years later, he gave me a gift: He had finished his college degree. He said, "Dad, we do not have much money. Four kids and college are not easy. However, I want you to know that here are my grades for my final semester. All As and one B." He had made the dean's list at the college he was attending! He is now filled with the Spirit and serves in ministry with young people—directing their lives toward victory.

Supply and Provision

I share this story because there are usually three areas in our life that require a faith breakthrough: family, provision and physical healing. The story of Joseph illustrates how the prayer of faith can work in our family, even though it may take many years to fully manifest. Let's first look at provision. Provision is a stock of needed materials or supplies. As we share in *Possessing Your Inheritance*, the word "provision" also means "to prepare to meet a need—to have it already stored up. God's vision and strategy carries with it the necessary provision; it is only a matter of bringing the revelation of release down on earth."[1] Provision is released when vision is fully defined.

Know that the Lord will provide for your vision.

I love the whole story about Elijah. In 1 Kings 17, we see his prayer lock up the heavens for three and a half years so that no rain fell. Elijah was fine for 40 days after making this declaration. He stayed by the Brook Cherith and had provision there. One key to seeing our provision is to be at the right place at the right time. He had water and food. However, his declaration of faith that had affected the heavens also affected him. The brook dried up! How many of us have ever had our provision dry up? When this happens, like Elijah, we need to gain new revelation from the Lord so that we can move forward.

Another key to God's provision is to watch for God's signs and supernatural connections along our paths. He sent Elijah to Zarephath and told him to look for a widow at the gate. When Elijah arrived, there she was, picking up sticks. He requested water and bread or a cake from her. It is important for you to be bold and ask for what you need.

Now let's turn and look at the widow. Notice her response in 1 Kings 17:12:

> As the LORD your God lives, I do not have bread, only a handful of flour in a bin, and a little oil in a jar; and see, I am gathering a couple of sticks that I may go in and prepare it for myself and my son, that we may eat it, and die.

How was that for a faith response? Things did not look good for Elijah. But God!

For our provision to be released, many times we must see what we already have in our hand. Elijah was filled with faith, but the widow was so overwhelmed with her circumstance that she could not see how to take what she had and multiply that for her future use. She had flour, oil and sticks. What makes bread? Flour, oil and fire. Once we start using what we have, the Lord begins to multiply our resources. The prayer of faith causes multiplication. When we are being tested in provision, we need to rise up, pray the prayer of faith and open our eyes to see the same way God sees.

Healing

The blood of Jesus, infused with the power to heal, is still as active today as ever. In fact, His blood will be active forever.

Psalm 107:20 reassures us: "He sent His word and healed them, and delivered them from their destructions." We are moving into a new dimension of healing. Each of us should ask his- or herself, *Do I know Him as Healer?* Anyone who does not should then ask, *How can I get to know Him as Healer?*

THE BLOOD OF JESUS, INFUSED WITH THE POWER TO HEAL, IS STILL AS ACTIVE TODAY AS EVER.

I have prayed for people and seen many instantly healed. I have prayed for others who have not been healed and some who have died. At times, I have been sick and then instantly healed. At other times, I have had to war for years to overcome certain infirmities. However, God is God. We should not get discouraged; rather, we must keep warring in faith and seeking Him for our next step of revelation.

And the prayer of faith will save the sick, and the Lord will raise him up. And if he has committed sins, he will be forgiven (Jas. 5:15).

Whether we are healed instantly or have to pray for years, the bottom line is that the prayer of faith heals the sick.

A Supernatural Dimension

> Then the LORD spoke to Moses and Aaron, saying, "When Pharaoh speaks to you, saying, 'Show a miracle for yourselves,' then you shall say to Aaron, 'Take your rod and cast it before Pharaoh, and let it become a serpent' " (Exod. 7:8-9).

These verses are very important. When God speaks to us, that gives us a reply to the enemy with whom we are contending!

A SELF-EVALUATION

Here are some questions and statements that can help evaluate where you are in outwitting your enemy.

1. What is your communication level with the Father?
2. Does your prayer life take on a supernatural dimension? Do you believe in the supernatural? Do you consider yourself operating in a supernatural dimension? Here are some words that are linked with the supernatural to help you think this through:

   - miracles
   - power
   - pictures of the throne room
   - spirit realm
   - faith
   - suddenlies
   - open heaven
   - demonstrations
   - angels

- ability to see into the unseen
- communications through dreams and visions
- discernment of spirits
- prophetic
- deliverance
- beyond human boundaries
- kingdom mentality

3. Write down five supernatural experiences you have had that you don't understand. Also ask yourself,

- When was the first time God spoke to me?
- How did He speak to me?
- When was the first time I was confronted by the enemy?
- How did he manifest himself?
- How did you respond to these supernatural events?

4. Do you know and have an intimate relationship with the Holy Spirit? You need to know the Person who is linking you into the supernatural! You should have the following goals if you intend to live and walk in a new supernatural dimension of prayer, faith and overcoming victory. You should seek to understand

- the Person of the Holy Spirit
- the Kingdom that we live in
- the apostolic government and authority
- the anointing
- the realm of faith
- glory

5. Do you understand that the enemy and his agents are set against you? These agents intervene supernaturally to stop you from entering into your abiding place and wearing a mantle of favor.

6. Do you believe in and attempt to discern and evaluate supernatural manifestations? Discernment will be key for you in evaluating:

- miracles
- signs and wonders
- symbols
- dreams
- visions
- faith

7. What will it take to move into this dimension?

- Break every limitation the enemy has put in your mind about the Holy Spirit. He has tried to keep you from knowing the Person of the Holy Spirit.
- Understand the times you are living in. Learn to recognize what the Holy Spirit is doing on Earth today.
- Enter into a new level of faith. Go from faith to faith. Let your faith increase.
- Understand the authority structure of which you are a part. What is the foundation on which you stand? With whom are you connected? How do you fit into the government around you? Faith works through authority (see Matt. 8).

- Define your connections at this point in your life and ministry. Who is shielding you, and who are you shielding? This is a major issue! Pray for those above and beneath you.
- Your willingness to worship and sacrifice in new ways must change. Know that giving + worship + authority = increased faith.
- What ceiling has been placed on your life that is limiting your breakthrough? How is the enemy limiting you? If you come into agreement with anything the enemy does in any area of your life, the result is oppression or depression.

To help you further understand vibrant faith that equips us for outwitting the enemy, Robert Heidler and I wrote *Restoring Your Shield of Faith*. There are many more principles covered in that book than we have been able to touch on in this short chapter.

Note

1. Chuck D. Pierce and Rebecca Wagner Sytsema, *Possessing Your Inheritance* (Ventura, CA: Renew, 1999), pp. 130-131.

CHAPTER 8

MOVING FORWARD!

At the time I wrote this book, the Lord had His finger on my son Isaac. One week, Isaac went with the youth group at church down to Big Bend National Park in West Texas. On that trip, Pam was one of the leaders. When I asked her how it went, she said everything was outstanding—except for one thing that Isaac could share with me. Isaac told me that the kids had gone into the river and he had forgotten to take out his wallet before going in. As a result, he lost his wallet in the river. "My Six Flags (amusement park) season pass was in there," he explained. "I'm supposed to go to Six Flags one more time this year, so you need to get me a new season pass along with the $76 that were in my wallet."

I could have replaced his wallet and its contents, but a good father knows that sometimes he must point his children to their heavenly Father. I told him that I would join him in praying for his wallet to be found and returned. Imagine that—someone's finding and returning his river-soaked wallet that had been lost in the Big Bend National Park. If that didn't sound silly enough, I then said that his mom would also help. Pam offered to call the warden and let him know about Isaac's lost wallet.

My son and I got down on our knees in his bedroom to pray for the return of his wallet. He prayed, "Lord, I lost my wallet in the river at Big Bend National Park. It's black with red flames on it and has a Six Flags season pass in it along with $76. I know I'm supposed to go to Six Flags one more time this summer, so I need Your help to get it back since my dad won't help me." Talk about shifting the blame to me! When he was done, he told me it was my turn to pray. All I could do was say, "Amen," and resist the urge to throttle him. But in saying "amen," I did sincerely come into agreement that his wallet be returned.

Several weeks later I was in Minnesota. While ministering on the platform, my cell phone rang with a call from my family. The game warden in Big Bend National Park had found Isaac's wallet and was returning it—with the money and Six Flags season pass still in it! Needless to say, my son immediately began to make plans for one last trip to the amusement park. What a poignant reminder this was to me of the power of two coming together in the prayer of agreement.

Again I say to you that if two of you agree on earth concerning anything that they ask, it will be done for them by My Father in heaven (Matt. 18:19).

THE PRAYER OF AGREEMENT

The Greek word for agree in this verse is *sumphoneo* which literally means "to sound together," to be harmonious.[1] Sounding together in prayer is very powerful and opens the windows of heaven. The Lord doesn't call us to stand alone in our struggle to outwit the enemy in our lives. We need others to come into agreement with us. Sometimes it is the only way we will see real

WE MUST NOT BE DISTRACTED BY THE MANY THINGS FOR WHICH WE COULD PRAY; RATHER, GOD HAS CERTAIN ASSIGNMENTS FOR EACH OF US.

breakthrough. In fact, we will not be able to fully overcome his schemes in our lives without the wisdom, counsel and intercessory prayer of those with whom God has connected us.

Furthermore, the Lord does not call us to focus only on that which concerns us. We are part of a Body, and there will be times when He calls upon us to agree with others over their struggles. Seeing the enemy outwitted applies to everything that opposes God and His purposes. That is what intercession is all about. Of course, we as individuals aren't called to pray over everything. In fact, we must not be distracted by the many things for which we *could* pray; rather, God has certain assignments for each of us.

We also need to be very open to His Spirit and understand that He may ask us to stand in the gap for an individual, a territory, an important issue or something else that is on His heart.

IN THE GAP

One of my roles has been to let the Lord give me assignments to fill a gap. This has meant everything from having a certain prayer emphasis to serving in an administrative role for various building projects.

In *Seasons of Intercession*, Pastor Frank Damazio explains the concept of gap standing.

> The word "gap" in the Hebrew means a rupture or breach. This word is taken from a military context, and applies to besiegers who rush into a city through breaches in the wall. The besieging army would attack one specific place in the wall until it was weakened. Then with united strength, the enemy would rush the wall, causing a break or breach. The gap standing soldier's responsibility was to risk his life by standing in the breach and single-handedly repelling the enemy. This was known to be one of the bravest acts of a soldier, since he risked severe injury and danger. Often these soldiers gave their lives to fill the gap and save the city. A gap standing soldier was a highly respected and sought out name among soldiers.[2]

A 50-State Tour

One gap-standing assignment in which I have been privileged to participate is called the 50-State Tour. One morning in October

2002, I awoke with a sense of urgency from the Lord. I sensed that I was to travel to all 50 of the United States to help raise up the prayer army of God in each state. The next time I was ministering with Dutch Sheets, who also has a heart for revival in our nation, I brought this up only to find that he had felt the same urgency the week before.

WE NEED TO PRAY AS JESUS TAUGHT US THAT HIS WILL WOULD BE DONE ON EARTH AS IT IS IN HEAVEN.

We could sense that the Lord was calling us to work together on this project. We called meetings to identify and draw together the intercessors of each state, and then align strategic intercession with apostolic, prophetic, pastoral leadership. As we have done this, we have seen God raise up an army in each state. This gap standing has produced amazing, miraculous results. We have seen God's prophetic anointing rise to new levels in ways that will move the Body of Christ forward to accomplish His purposes in each territory.

God has a way of seeing His will accomplished on Earth. We each play a part in this process. We need to pray as Jesus taught us that His will would be done on Earth as it is in heaven. This begins when He releases His burden from heaven. One of the phrases related to intercession is "burden bearing," which means to sustain, bear or hold up against a thing. Dutch Sheets wrote, "This is likened to when a person will tie a stake to a tomato plant to sustain it from the weight it carries. The strength of the stake is transferred to the plant, and thus, 'bears' it up."[3] Sheets also wrote that another word for burden is " 'to bear, lift or carry' something with the idea being to carry it *away* or *remove* it. . . . The intercessory work of Christ reached its fullest and most profound expression when our sins were 'laid on' Him and He bore 'them' away."[4] Similarly, the Lord will lay His burden on us for something He wants removed, and we are to stand in the gap and pray until we get rid of it.

THE BUILDING PLAN

The Lord calls us not only to tear down but also to build up. Nehemiah was a great example of one who stood in the gap and sought to see the foundations of Jerusalem restored. He was one of the Jews of the dispersion, and in his youth was appointed to the important office of royal cupbearer at the palace of Shushan. Through his brother Hanani, and perhaps from other sources, he heard of the mournful and desolate condition of the Holy City, and was filled with sadness of heart (see Neh. 1:2; 2:3). The king observed his countenance and asked the reason for it. Nehemiah explained it all to the king and obtained his permission to go up to Jerusalem and act as the governor of Judea.

Upon his arrival, he set himself to survey the city and to form a plan for its restoration. However, the enemies of the Jews had no intention of allowing the walls of Jerusalem to be repaired. From the moment of Nehemiah's arrival in Judea, Sanballat, whose name means bramble-bush or enemy-in-secret, set himself to oppose every measure for the restoration of Jerusalem's security. Sanballat was "the man" that Nehemiah had to overcome. Sanballat's opposition was confined at first to scoffs and insults, and he circulated all sorts of disparaging reflections that might increase feelings of hatred and contempt amongst Nehemiah's colleagues. However, Nehemiah prayed to the Lord that the enemy's insults would be turned back on his head, and the rebuilding continued until the wall reached half its projected height.

When Sanballat and his coalition saw that Nehemiah had reached the halfway point in the reconstruction, Sanballat staged another attack. He formed a conspiracy to surprise the Jews, demolish their work and disperse or intimidate the builders. From this it is important for us to recognize that the enemy cannot afford to allow our building plan to succeed. And if his initial strategy to thwart our efforts fails, he will regroup and try again—just as Sanballat did. However, Sanballat's plot was discovered, and Nehemiah adopted measures for ensuring the common safety as well as the uninterrupted building of the walls. Now half of the laborers were withdrawn to be constantly in arms. The workmen labored with a trowel in one hand and a sword in the other. Nehemiah also kept a trumpeter by his side, so that when any intelligence of a surprise was brought to him, an alarm could immediately be sounded. This would allow assistance to go wherever it was needed. By these precautions, the plans of the enemy were defeated. By seeking the Lord, Nehemiah executed a building plan and saw that the wall was completed.

GET PAST YOUR HALFWAY POINT

So we built the wall, and all of it was joined together to half its height, for the people had a heart and mind to work! (Neh. 4:6, *Amp.*).

When I read this the Lord said, *Tell My people to get past the half-way mark.* What does it take to get past the *halfway* mark and move forward? Here are 12 steps to get us to the other side. Most of these issues have been discussed throughout this book.

1. **Overcome accusations.** The accuser tries to stop us. False judgments lead to delays.
2. **Understand the conspiracy set against us.** The enemy does not play fair. He tries to mobilize others to help him stop God's covenant blessing.
3. **Break a demeaning spirit against what we are building.** If accusations don't stop us, he will try to place worthlessness upon what we are accomplishing. Break a power of worthlessness.
4. **Enter into a new dimension of bold praying and define our gaps.** Nehemiah prayed differently. He said, "Lord, blot out the enemies!" Let's get bold in our praying.
5. **Break legalistic structures.** The enemy always tries to change laws and times. He will develop a legalistic structure to restrain our movement.
6. **Receive a new dimension of faith.** Decree that **GOD IS ABLE** for us to accomplish our goal and get to our destination.
7. **Evaluate those who are building with us.** Many times the Lord wants us to review who is with us and what supernatural connections we need to move forward.
8. **Get a new force of intercession in place.** We need to close the gaps. Therefore, we must be sure to have an intercessory force surrounding what we are doing.
9. **Review our war strategy.** We need a strategy or set

of plans to overcome the conflicts set against us. We also have to have God's blueprint to build His way.

10. **Find prophetic input.** We always need to know the prophetic trumpet to which we are listening. Without a vision, or prophetic revelation, a people perish, and so does a project.

11. **See how to become better connected and to communicate in a more efficient way.** Sometimes communication is our downfall. Let's ask the Lord to streamline our process and make all communication efficient.

12. **Go past our halfway point!** Declare that we are headed to the other side.

THE GOAL

Once we get past the halfway point, we need a strategy to complete the assignment. This can be likened to a project. Looking at our assignments from the Lord in that light, here is a plan to help us complete our projects:

- **Project background.** Always review what has already happened.
- **Project problem statement.** Just as Nehemiah did, define the problems related to the project.
- **Project opportunity statement.** Write out how this project will open windows of opportunity in the future.
- **Project resource availability.** Analyze all resources to see what is available.
- **Project resource need.** Analyze the project to determine

what resources are needed. Without doing this properly and getting prayer in place, many times we cannot
acquire the necessary resources to complete the project, and we become frustrated.

- **Project time constraints.** We must stay in God's
  perfect time plan. Look at the time constraints. By
  walking in God's timeframe, we defeat the plan of
  the enemy.
- **Project benefits.** We should always keep an eye on
  the benefits of each project. This will help our faith
  move up a level.

God is ready and able to work on our behalf. Whether He
calls us to stand and watch His salvation occur, or calls us to
engage the enemy, wielding our swords, God has a victory plan
for us, and it is He who will ultimately outwit and defeat our
enemy. We must seek the Lord, gain strategic revelation for moving forward, be obedient to His commands and let Him handle
the rest for us: " 'Not by might nor by power, but by My Spirit,'
says the LORD of hosts" (Zech. 4:6). Let us always remember that
when it looks as though we have been defeated, the King has one
more move!

Notes
1. Biblesoft's New Exhaustive Strong's Numbers and Concordance with
   Expanded Greek-Hebrew Dictionary. Copyright © 1994, 2003 Biblesoft,
   Inc. and International Bible Translators, Inc.
2. Frank Damazio, *Seasons of Intercession* (Portland, OR: City Bible
   Publishing, 1998), pp. 113-114.
3. Dutch Sheets, *Intercessory Prayer* (Ventura, CA: Regal Books, 1996), p. 62.
4. Ibid., pp. 62-63.

32-DAY PRAYER FOCUS TO ESTABLISH A REARGUARD

It is time to put into action the strategies outlined in this book. This appendix walks you through 32 days of prayer to establish your rearguard. Each day, start by reading the specific Scripture we have selected. Most days, we have provided the entire reading. On a few days, we ask you to read a whole chapter, so you will need your Bible. After the Scripture excerpt comes an action point for you to focus on or instill in your life. Finally, pray. This is not something to be done by rote. You cannot skip over it, because it is vital to establishing your rearguard. This is not a book just about prayer concepts; it is also an action plan. Pray through each Scripture. Take notes. In the space provided, record what you have prayed and what you hear from God. In 32 days you will have fully established your rearguard and will be constantly outwitting the enemy along the way.

DAY 1

Then all the tribes of Israel came to David at Hebron and spoke, saying, "Indeed we are your bone and your flesh. Also, in time past, when Saul was king over us, you were the one who led Israel out and brought them in; and the LORD said to you, 'You shall shepherd My people Israel, and be ruler over Israel.'" Therefore all the elders of Israel came to the king at Hebron, and King David made a covenant with them at Hebron before the LORD. And they anointed David king over Israel. David was thirty years old when he began to reign, and he reigned forty years. In Hebron he reigned over Judah seven years and six months, and in Jerusalem he reigned thirty-three years over all Israel and Judah.

2 SAMUEL 5:1-5

ACTION POINT

Receive a new anointing. The Lord is bringing a new anointing to His people. That anointing will cause prophetic words that have lain dormant to begin to be activated in the atmosphere. The anointing breaks the yoke. Go where the anointing is moving and have a receptive heart.

PRAYER NOTES

PRAYER FOCUS

DAY 2

And the king and his men went to Jerusalem against the Jebusites, the inhabitants of the land, who spoke to David, saying, "You shall not come in here; but the blind and the lame will repel you," thinking, "David cannot come in here." Nevertheless David took the stronghold of Zion (that is, the City of David).

2 SAMUEL 5:6-7

ACTION POINT

Allow the Lord to show you iniquitous patterns that are hanging around in your life. God had wanted the Jebusites to be overthrown when Canaan was taken. This was written around 400 years later and 800 years from the time that the Lord first covenanted with Abraham to bring down the Jebusites. The Lord does not forget an old, iniquitous pattern that would weaken you.

PRAYER NOTES

PRAYER FOCUS

DAY 3

Now David said on that day, "Whoever climbs up by way of the water shaft and defeats the Jebusites (the lame and the blind, who are hated by David's soul), he shall be chief and captain." Therefore they say, "The blind and the lame shall not come into the house."

Then David dwelt in the stronghold, and called it the City of David. And David built all around from the Millo and inward. So David went on and became great, and the LORD God of hosts was with him.

Then Hiram king of Tyre sent messengers to David, and cedar trees, and carpenters and masons. And they built David a house. So David knew that the LORD had established him as king over Israel, and that He had exalted His kingdom for the sake of His people Israel.

And David took more concubines and wives from Jerusalem, after he had come from Hebron. Also more sons and daughters were born to David. Now these are the names of those who were born to him in Jerusalem: Shammua, Shobab, Nathan, Solomon, Ibhar, Elishua, Nepheg, Japhia, Elishama, Eliada, and Eliphelet.

2 SAMUEL 5:8-16

ACTION POINT

Open your eyes and you will see the path that leads to victory. If you come into a new place of intimacy and communion with God, your eyes will open to see new strategies to break the enemy's power. Don't be afraid to get your knees dirty. Crawl through that narrow place and surprise your enemy.

PRAYER NOTES

PRAYER FOCUS

DAY 4

Now when the Philistines heard that they had anointed David king over Israel, all the Philistines went up to search for David. So David inquired of the LORD, saying, "Shall I go up against the Philistines? Will You deliver them into my hand?" And the LORD said to David, "Go up, for I will doubtless deliver the Philistines into your hand."

2 SAMUEL 5:17,19

ACTION POINT

Don't allow the enemy's backlash to get you off course. Many of God's people begin to have victory and then fall short. The enemy sees your new anointing and then raises up new forces to come against you. When you sense this backlash or retaliation once you are having victory, don't let fear engulf you. Stop and pray. Just as David did, ask the Lord if you are to war or to wait. If you hear Him say, "War!" then do it!

PRAYER NOTES

PRAYER FOCUS

DAY 5

So David went to Baal Perazim, and David defeated them there;
and he said, "The LORD has broken through my enemies before me, like
a breakthrough of water." Therefore he called the name of that place
Baal Perazim. And they left their images there, and David and
his men carried them away.

2 SAMUEL 5:20-21

ACTION POINT

Declare deliverance and breakthrough throughout this day.
Outline your Baal Perazims. Declare that the Master of Breakthrough will rise on your behalf. Ask for a new anointing of
intercession.

PRAYER NOTES

PRAYER FOCUS

DAY 6

*Then the Philistines went up once again and deployed themselves
in the Valley of Rephaim. Therefore David inquired of the LORD, and
He said, "You shall not go up; circle around behind them, and come
upon them in front of the mulberry trees."*

2 SAMUEL 5:22-23

ACTION POINT

Don't drop your shield until you see your enemy completely pushed back.
The Philistines returned with another counterattack. Even after
victory occurs, stay alert to the enemy's location. Any time you
discern the enemy's presence, inquire of the Lord. Much creativity
is needed to utterly defeat the enemy. Yesterday you had
God's strategy and direction; today He has a new path for you to
take. God is faithful morning by morning. Gain your direction
daily. See your enemy that is encroached upon your territory
totally removed.

PRAYER NOTES
DAY 6

PRAYER FOCUS

DAY 7

And it shall be, when you hear the sound of marching in the tops of the mulberry trees, then you shall advance quickly. For then the LORD will go out before you to strike the camp of the Philistines.

2 SAMUEL 5:24

ACTION POINT

Wait for the sound of the Holy Spirit in your midst. The Holy Spirit is breathing a new, fresh sound for victory. If you miss His sound, it will take you out of God's timing in facing off the enemy. Hear the sound of the Spirit of God.

PRAYER NOTES

PRAYER FOCUS

DAY 8

And David did so, as the LORD commanded him; and he drove
back the Philistines from Geba as far as Gezer.

2 SAMUEL 5:25

ACTION POINT

Declare everything in your land—life, home, church, city and nation—to
be secured. David secured his covenant territory. We need to do
the same with ours.

PRAYER NOTES

DAY 9

Again David gathered all the choice men of Israel, thirty thousand. And David arose and went with all the people who were with him from Baale Judah to bring up from there the ark of God, whose name is called by the Name, the LORD of Hosts, who dwells between the cherubim. So they set the ark of God on a new cart, and brought it out of the house of Abinadab, which was on the hill; and Uzzah and Ahio, the sons of Abinadab, drove the new cart. And they brought it out of the house of Abinadab, which was on the hill, accompanying the ark of God; and Ahio went before the ark.

Then David and all the house of Israel played music before the LORD on all kinds of instruments of fir wood, on harps, on stringed instruments, on tambourines, on sistrums, and on cymbals.
And when they came to Nachon's threshing floor, Uzzah put out his hand to the ark of God and took hold of it, for the oxen stumbled. Then the anger of the LORD was aroused against Uzzah, and God struck him there for his error; and he died there by the ark of God. And David became angry because of the LORD's outbreak against Uzzah; and he called the name of the place Perez Uzzah to this day.

David was afraid of the LORD that day; and he said, "How can the ark of the LORD come to me?" So David would not move the ark of the LORD with him into the City of David; but David took it aside into the house of Obed-Edom the Gittite. The ark of the LORD remained in the house of Obed-Edom the Gittite three months. And the LORD blessed Obed-Edom and all his household.

Now it was told King David, saying, "The LORD has blessed the house of
Obed-Edom and all that belongs to him, because of the ark of God." So
David went and brought up the ark of God from the house of Obed-
Edom to the City of David with gladness. And so it was, when those
bearing the ark of the LORD had gone six paces, that he sacrificed
oxen and fatted sheep. Then David danced before the LORD with
all his might; and David was wearing a linen ephod. So David and
all the house of Israel brought up the ark of the LORD with
shouting and with the sound of the trumpet.

Now as the ark of the LORD came into the City of David, Michal, Saul's
daughter, looked through a window and saw King David leaping and
whirling before the LORD; and she despised him in her heart. So they
brought the ark of the LORD, and set it in its place in the midst of the
tabernacle that David had erected for it. Then David offered burnt offerings and peace offerings before the LORD. And when David had finished
offering burnt offerings and peace offerings, he blessed the people in the
name of the LORD of hosts. Then he distributed among all the people,
among the whole multitude of Israel, both the women and the men, to
everyone a loaf of bread, a piece of meat, and a cake of raisins.
So all the people departed, everyone to his house.

Then David returned to bless his household. And Michal the daughter of
Saul came out to meet David, and said, "How glorious was the king of
Israel today, uncovering himself today in the eyes of the maids of his
servants, as one of the base fellows shamelessly uncovers himself!"

So David said to Michal, "It was before the LORD, who chose me
instead of your father and all his house, to appoint me ruler over the people of the LORD, over Israel. Therefore I will play music before the
LORD. And I will be even more undignified than this, and will
be humble in my own sight. But as for the maidservants of

whom you have spoken, by them I will be held in honor."

*Therefore Michal the daughter of Saul had no children
to the day of her death.*

2 SAMUEL 6

ACTION POINT

Worship and establish God's presence in your midst. After a false start, David brought the Ark back as the central force of all of Israel. We need to recognize any false starts we have made and abide in a place of worship before God.

PRAYER NOTES

PRAYER FOCUS

DAY 10

Now, O LORD God, the word which You have spoken concerning Your servant and concerning his house, establish it forever and do as You have said. So let Your name be magnified forever, saying, "The LORD of hosts is the God over Israel." And let the house of Your servant David be established before You. For You, O LORD of hosts, God of Israel, have revealed this to Your servant, saying, "I will build you a house." Therefore Your servant has found it in his heart to pray this prayer to You.

And now, O Lord God, You are God, and Your words are true, and You have promised this goodness to Your servant. Now therefore, let it please You to bless the house of Your servant, that it may continue before You forever; for You, O Lord God, have spoken it, and with Your blessing let the house of Your servant be blessed forever.

2 SAMUEL 7:25-29

ACTION POINT

Declare: The Lord will establish my house! Pray for your house. Also pray for the church or ministry to which you are most connected.

PRAYER NOTES

DAY 11

After this it came to pass that David attacked the Philistines and subdued them. And David took Metheg Ammah from the hand of the Philistines.

Then he defeated Moab. Forcing them down to the ground, he measured them off with a line. With two lines he measured off those to be put to death, and with one full line those to be kept alive. So the Moabites became David's servants, and brought tribute.

David also defeated Hadadezer the son of Rehob, king of Zobah, as he went to recover his territory at the River Euphrates. David took from him one thousand chariots, seven hundred horsemen, and twenty thousand foot soldiers. Also David hamstrung all the chariot horses, except that he spared enough of them for one hundred chariots.

When the Syrians of Damascus came to help Hadadezer king of Zobah, David killed twenty-two thousand of the Syrians. Then David put garrisons in Syria of Damascus; and the Syrians became David's servants, and brought tribute. So the LORD preserved David wherever he went. And David took the shields of gold that had belonged to the servants of Hadadezer, and brought them to Jerusalem. Also from Betah and from Berothai, cities of Hadadezer, King David took a large amount of bronze.

When Toi king of Hamath heard that David had defeated all the army of Hadadezer, then Toi sent Joram his son to King David, to greet him and bless him, because he had fought against Hadadezer and defeated him (for Hadadezer had been at war with Toi); and Joram brought with him articles of silver, articles of gold, and articles of bronze. King David also dedicated these to the LORD, along with the silver and gold that he had dedicated from all the nations which he had subdued—12 from Syria, from Moab, from the people of Ammon, from the Philistines, from Amalek, and from the spoil of Hadadezer the son of Rehob, king of Zobah.

And David made himself a name when he returned from killing eighteen thousand Syrians in the Valley of Salt. He also put garrisons in Edom; throughout all Edom he put garrisons, and all the Edomites became David's servants. And the LORD preserved David wherever he went.

2 SAMUEL 8:1-14

ACTION POINT

Declare that you will take hold of that which is leading you, and that instead of being led, you will lead forth in God's purposes. David took Metheg Ammah. This means the bridle of the mother city. Once the presence of God was established, David actually took the stronghold of the Philistines. What strongholds do we need to take?

PRAYER NOTES

PRAYER FOCUS

DAY 12

Awake, awake!
Put on your strength, O Zion;
Put on your beautiful garments,
O Jerusalem, the holy city!
For the uncircumcised and the unclean
Shall no longer come to you.
Shake yourself from the dust, arise;
Sit down, O Jerusalem!
Loose yourself from the bonds of your neck,
O captive daughter of Zion!
For thus says the LORD:
"You have sold yourselves for nothing,
And you shall be redeemed without money."
For thus says the Lord GOD:
"My people went down at first
Into Egypt to dwell there;
Then the Assyrian oppressed them without cause.
Now therefore, what have I here," says the LORD,
"That My people are taken away for nothing?
Those who rule over them
Make them wail," says the LORD,
"And My name is blasphemed continually every day.
Therefore My people shall know My name;
Therefore they shall know in that day
That I am He who speaks:
'Behold, it is I.'"
How beautiful upon the mountains

Are the feet of him who brings good news,
Who proclaims peace,
Who brings glad tidings of good things,
Who proclaims salvation,
Who says to Zion,
"Your God reigns!"
Your watchmen shall lift up their voices,
With their voices they shall sing together;
For they shall see eye to eye
When the LORD brings back Zion.
Break forth into joy, sing together,
You waste places of Jerusalem!
For the LORD has comforted His people,
He has redeemed Jerusalem.
The LORD has made bare His holy arm
In the eyes of all the nations;
And all the ends of the earth shall see
The salvation of our God.
Depart! Depart! Go out from there,
Touch no unclean thing;
Go out from the midst of her,
Be clean,
You who bear the vessels of the LORD.
For you shall not go out with haste,
Nor go by flight;
For the LORD will go before you,
And the God of Israel will be your rear guard.
Behold, My Servant shall deal prudently;
He shall be exalted and extolled and be very high.
Just as many were astonished at you,
So His visage was marred more than any man,
And His form more than the sons of men;

So shall He sprinkle many nations.
Kings shall shut their mouths at Him;
For what had not been told them they shall see,
And what they had not heard they shall consider.

ISAIAH 52

ACTION POINT

Receive a new strength. Your strength to withstand the attack of the enemy is something that you actually have to put on. You must review the condition of your armor and repair every place that has been weakened through apathy or a spirit of slumber. This can rob you of strength. You need to order your prayers, gain strategy and allow your steps to be ordered of the Lord. In doing so, you will gain the necessary strength for the war that lies ahead.

PRAYER NOTES

PRAYER FOCUS

DAY 13

With whom My hand shall be established; also My arm
shall strengthen him.

PSALM 89:21

ACTION POINT

There is a new strength. Strength means to have power, vigor, might, energy and fervency. But another definition of strength is to have power by reason of influence, authority or resources. Like anointing, our covenant with God positions us for strength over the enemy by the very influence, authority and resources available to us. Strength also means power to withstand an attack.

PRAYER NOTES

PRAYER FOCUS

DAY 14

The enemy shall not outwit him, nor the son of wickedness afflict him.

PSALM 89:22

ACTION POINT

Declare that any plan the enemy has set against you will be found out and seen. Read all of Psalm 89. We will not be outwitted by the enemy. The literal meaning of this verse has to do with demanding a debt be paid without showing mercy. Because you have a covenant position with God, in this case standing clean and blameless before Him through the blood of Jesus, you are not indebted to the enemy, and therefore, you need not be outwitted nor afflicted by him.

PRAYER NOTES

DAY 15

Therefore Jesus said again, "I tell you the truth, I am the gate for the sheep. All who ever came before me were thieves and robbers, but the sheep did not listen to them. I am the gate; whoever enters through me will be saved. He will come in and go out, and find pasture. The thief comes only to steal and kill and destroy; I have come that they may have life, and have it to the full.

"I am the good shepherd. The good shepherd lays down his life for the sheep. The hired hand is not the shepherd who owns the sheep. So when he sees the wolf coming, he abandons the sheep and runs away. Then the wolf attacks the flock and scatters it. The man runs away because he is a hired hand and cares nothing for the sheep.

"I am the good shepherd; I know my sheep and my sheep know me—just as the Father knows me and I know the Father—and I lay down my life for the sheep. I have other sheep that are not of this sheep pen. I must bring them also. They too will listen to my voice, and there shall be one flock and one shepherd. The reason my Father loves me is that I lay down my life—only to take it up again. No one takes it from me, but I lay it down of my own accord. I have authority to lay it down and authority to take it up again. This command I received from my Father."

JOHN 10:7-18, *NIV*

ACTION POINT

Declare that the thief will have no power over you. You have the power to outwit the enemy because of what he is attempting to steal from you. He is, therefore, in debt to you and because of your covenant position you have a right to fight him from that position and demand back what is yours through strategic prayer.

PRAYER NOTES

PRAYER FOCUS

DAY 16

I will beat down his foes before his face, and plague those who hate him.
PSALM 89:23

ACTION POINT

Praise God that He will take a stand on your behalf. Read all of Psalm 89. Once you are in covenant with the Lord, He displays Himself to overthrow the power of the enemy on your behalf.

PRAYER NOTES

PRAYER FOCUS

DAY 17

*So shall they fear the name of the LORD from the west, and His glory
from the rising of the sun; when the enemy comes in like a flood, the
Spirit of the LORD will lift up a standard against him.*

ISAIAH 59:19

ACTION POINT

Let the Lord raise His standard against your enemies. A standard was
considered in Old Testament times as a token of protection and
fidelity. According to the *New Unger's Bible Dictionary*, God's lift-
ing or setting up a standard implies a peculiar presence, protection and aid in leading and directing His people in the execution
of His righteous will and giving them comfort and peace in His
service. This covenant with the Lord positions you under this
powerful standard.

PRAYER NOTES

PRAYER FOCUS

DAY 18

Finally, be strong in the Lord and in his mighty power. Put on the full armor of God so that you can take your stand against the devil's schemes. For our struggle is not against flesh and blood, but against the rulers, against the authorities, against the powers of this dark world and against the spiritual forces of evil in the heavenly realms. Therefore put on the full armor of God, so that when the day of evil comes, you may be able to stand your ground, and after you have done everything, to stand.

EPHESIANS 6:10-13, *NIV*

ACTION POINT

Put on the whole armor of God. Position yourself for faith against any evil that might surround you. Hold at bay or stand in front of and oppose in active battle the enemy that has been taunting you. Take your stand for the next battle.

PRAYER NOTES

PRAYER FOCUS

DAY 19

Stand firm then, with the belt of truth buckled around your waist, with the breastplate of righteousness in place, and with your feet fitted with the readiness that comes from the gospel of peace. In addition to all this, take up the shield of faith, with which you can extinguish all the flaming arrows of the evil one. Take the helmet of salvation and the sword of the Spirit, which is the word of God. And pray in the Spirit on all occasions with all kinds of prayers and requests. With this in mind, be alert and always keep on praying for all the saints.

Pray also for me, that whenever I open my mouth, words may be given me so that I will fearlessly make known the mystery of the gospel, for which I am an ambassador in chains. Pray that I may declare it fearlessly, as I should.

EPHESIANS 6:14-20, *NIV*

ACTION POINT

Get your back side covered with the glory of God. The armor God has supplied to His New Testament soldiers does not provide for protection of the back of the warrior outside of the intercession of others. This is also consistent with the armies of Old Testament Israel where the "glory of the Lord" was to be their rearguard (see Isa. 58:8).

PRAYER NOTES

PRAYER FOCUS

DAY 20

Reread Ephesians 6:13 (see Day 18).

ACTION POINT

Withstand any attempt of the enemy's plans against you. To withstand is to *anthistemi.* The word "withstand" comes from the same word as "antihistamine." It means to vigorously oppose, bravely resist, stand face to face—just as an antihistamine puts a block on a histamine. Declare a new resistance to be built within you. Ask God to show you any place where your resistance has been torn down.

PRAYER NOTES

DAY 21

And the captain of the guard charged Joseph with them, and he served
them; so they were in custody for a while. Then the butler and the baker
of the king of Egypt, who were confined in the prison, had a dream, both
of them, each man's dream in one night and each man's dream with
its own interpretation. And Joseph came in to them in the morning
and looked at them, and saw that they were sad.

GENESIS 40:4-6

ACTION POINT

Declare vindication from your enemy. Read Genesis 49:16-17,
Exodus 30:6 and Numbers 2:25-31. The tribe of Dan served as a
rearguard to the north for all of Israel. Dan means vindication.
"[He] will be a serpent by the roadside, a viper along the path,
that bites the horse's heels so that its rider tumbles backward"
(Gen. 49:17, *NIV*). When operating in rearguard prayer, we
ambush our enemy and cause our enemy to stop pursuit and
actually lose strength.

PRAYER NOTES

PRAYER FOCUS

DAY 22

And Leah's maid Zilpah bore Jacob a second son. Then Leah said,
"I am happy, for the daughters will call me blessed."
So she called his name Asher.

GENESIS 30:12-13

ACTION POINT

Prepare a special offering for the King. Read Genesis 49:20 and
Deuteronomy 33:24-25. May your feet be anointed and shod
with the preparation of the Gospel of Peace. May you be ready to
accomplish anything God tells you. Receive new favor and
anointing for your steps to move forward. The tribe of Asher
also served as the rearguard. Asher means happy and fortunate.
Ask the Lord for new joy to move forward. Asher is linked with
favor and blessing. Asher fought with Gideon and pursued
Midian. Anna was of the tribe of Asher (see Luke 2:36). Wait
patiently until you see a manifestation of the promise. As you
give your offering, declare that you will hit a deep well of financial release.

PRAYER NOTES

PRAYER FOCUS

DAY 23

And Rachel's maid Bilhah conceived again and bore Jacob a second son.
Then Rachel said, "With great wrestlings I have wrestled with my sister,
and indeed I have prevailed." So she called his name Naphtali.

GENESIS 30:7-8

ACTION POINT

Gain strength to wrestle your enemies to the ground. Put your feet on
the head of your enemies. Read Genesis 30:7-8, Genesis 49:21
and Deuteronomy 33:23. Naphtali was also a rearguard tribe.
Naphtali means to wrestle. Wrestle over your promises.

PRAYER NOTES

PRAYER FOCUS

DAY 24

Now Deborah, a prophetess, the wife of Lapidoth, was judging Israel at that time. And she would sit under the palm tree of Deborah between Ramah and Bethel in the mountains of Ephraim. And the children of Israel came up to her for judgment. Then she sent and called for Barak the son of Abinoam from Kedesh in Naphtali, and said to him, "Has not the LORD God of Israel commanded, 'Go and deploy troops at Mount Tabor; take with you ten thousand men of the sons of Naphtali and of the sons of Zebulun; and against you I will deploy Sisera, the commander of Jabin's army, with his chariots and his multitude at the River Kishon; and I will deliver him into your hand'?"

JUDGES 4:4-7

ACTION POINT

Align yourself with those in your area who are warring for their inheritance. War alongside them, that you might obtain your inheritance. Read Judges 4 and Judges 6. See the example of how Naphtali fought with Barak and Gideon.

PRAYER NOTES
DAY 24

PRAYER FOCUS

DAY 25

And they helped David against the bands of raiders, for they were all mighty men of valor, and they were captains in the army. For at that time they came to David day by day to help him, until it was a great army, like the army of God.

1 CHRONICLES 12:21-22

ACTION POINT

Declare that the army of God will begin to grow. Read 1 Chronicles 12. Declare that the armies of heaven and Earth begin to agree. Ask for the Host of Heaven to be our rearguard. In 1 Chronicles 12:40, Naphtali brought food and provisions to the men of war at Hebron. Celebrate the King's coming into your territory, and declare abundant provision for the leadership of the Church to advance God's kingdom at this time.

PRAYER NOTES

PRAYER FOCUS

DAY 26

Then David consulted with the captains of thousands and hundreds, and with every leader. And David said to all the assembly of Israel, "If it seems good to you, and if it is of the LORD our God, let us send out to our brethren everywhere who are left in all the land of Israel, and with them to the priests and Levites who are in their cities and their common- lands, that they may gather together to us; and let us bring the ark of our God back to us, for we have not inquired at it since the days of Saul." Then all the assembly said that they would do so, for the thing was right in the eyes of all the people. So David gathered all Israel together, from Shihor in Egypt to as far as the entrance of Hamath, to bring the ark of God from Kirjath Jearim.

1 CHRONICLES 13:1-5

ACTION POINT

Pray that the presence of God be established anew and afresh in the nation. Read 1 Chronicles 13. The rearguard was positioned to protect the nation and the Ark.

PRAYER NOTES

PRAYER FOCUS

DAY 27

Now the LORD spoke to Moses, saying: "Speak to the children of Israel, that they turn and camp before Pi Hahiroth, between Migdol and the sea, opposite Baal Zephon; you shall camp before it by the sea. For Pharaoh will say of the children of Israel, 'They are bewildered by the land; the wilderness has closed them in.' Then I will harden Pharaoh's heart, so that he will pursue them; and I will gain honor over Pharaoh and over all his army, that the Egyptians may know that I am the LORD." And they did so.

EXODUS 14:1-4

ACTION POINT

Declare that every Pharaoh spirit you are aware of will let go. Read Exodus 14. Allow God to establish His glory. Press out of your bondage and allow God to establish His glory behind you. Set your heart to worship differently. God's people wanted Pharaoh to let them go so that they could worship in a new way. Find some new way to worship differently, and cast aside everything that would prevent you from it.

PRAYER NOTES

PRAYER FOCUS

DAY 28

"And now, O priests, this commandment is for you.
If you will not hear,
And if you will not take it to heart,
To give glory to My name,"
Says the LORD of hosts,
"I will send a curse upon you,
And I will curse your blessings.
Yes, I have cursed them already,
Because you do not take it to heart."

MALACHI 2:1-2

ACTION POINT

Give God all the glory for what He has done in your life. Take the words from Malachi to heart to give God the glory for all He has done in your life so that you might advance into His covenant blessings.

PRAYER NOTES

DAY 29

The LORD said to Joshua: "See! I have given Jericho into your hand, its king, and the mighty men of valor. You shall march around the city, all you men of war; you shall go all around the city once. This you shall do six days."

JOSHUA 6:2-3

ACTION POINT

Do a Jericho march, even if it's in your prayer closet. Read Joshua 6. Ask God for quietness and confidence against your enemy. Do not release a victory shout until His perfect time.

PRAYER NOTES

PRAYER FOCUS

DAY 30

Thus says the LORD of hosts, the God of Israel, to all who were carried away captive, whom I have caused to be carried away from Jerusalem to Babylon:
Build houses and dwell in them; plant gardens and eat their fruit. Take wives and beget sons and daughters; and take wives for your sons and give your daughters to husbands, so that they may bear sons and daughters—that you may be increased there, and not diminished. And seek the peace of the city where I have caused you to be carried away captive, and pray to the LORD for it; for in its peace you will have peace.
JEREMIAH 29:4-7

ACTION POINT

Pray for the peace of your city. Read Joshua 6 again, along with Jeremiah 29. Declare that any invincible force in your city will fall. Declare wholeness over your city.

PRAYER NOTES

PRAYER FOCUS

DAY 31

For you shall not go out with haste,
Nor go by flight;
For the LORD go before you,
And the God of Israel will be your rear guard.

ISAIAH 52:12

ACTION POINT

Declare God's perfect timing over your life. Memorize Isaiah 52:12. Declare that God's redemptive work through Jesus Christ will come in new fullness in your life. "For you shall not go out with haste nor go by flight; for the LORD will go before you, and the God of Israel will be your rear guard!" Wait on the Lord. Let your feet be put in His perfect timing. Order your prayers. Write them on a sheet of paper. Once you have ordered your prayers, let Him order your feet.

PRAYER NOTES

PRAYER FOCUS

DAY 32

So it was, whenever the ark set out, that Moses said:
"Rise up, O LORD!
Let Your enemies be scattered,
And let those who hate You flee before You."
NUMBERS 10:35

ACTION POINT

Let the trumpet sound. Hear the sound coming forth for war. Read Numbers 10. Move forth in God's order of victory. Declare the leadership of your church or ministry connection freshly established. Declare the leadership of this nation fully in order. War is on the horizon. Depart from the place at which you have settled. Go forth and know that God already has the victory plan.

PRAYER NOTES

WARRING WITH A PROPHETIC WORD

This charge I commit to you, son Timothy, according to the
prophecies previously made concerning you, that by them
you may wage the good warfare.

1 TIMOTHY 1:18

We have talked a great deal about destiny and prophetic fulfillment, but we have not discussed prophecy itself. This chapter is devoted to understanding the role that prophecy plays in our lives, and how to wage warfare with the prophecies we receive.

UNDERSTANDING PERSONAL PROPHECY

The simple definition of prophecy is speaking forth the mind and heart of God under the inspiration of the Holy Spirit. Therefore, to give an accurate word of God we must have both His mind and emotion as we deliver that word. A prophetic declaration communicates God's intent to fulfill His promises to us. Receiving a prophetic word can have a powerful impact on the perception of our prophetic destiny. This word can help shape our vision for the future and bring us into a deeper understanding of God's heart for our lives.

In our book *Receiving the Word of the Lord*, we discuss more fully the value, process and function of prophecy, and offer several ways to test a prophetic word. That book will help anyone needing a basic explanation of personal prophecy. In the context of this book, however, we want to focus on prophecy as it pertains to prophetic fulfillment. To do that, we need to take a closer look at several aspects of how prophecy works in our lives.[1]

Prophecy Is Incomplete

"For we know in part and we prophesy in part" (1 Cor. 13:9). No personal or corporate word of prophecy is complete in and of itself. In his excellent book, *Developing Your Prophetic Gifting*, Graham Cooke says, "God only reveals what we need to know in order to do his will in that particular time and place. The things that he does not wish us to know, he keeps secret from the one prophesying. Elisha said, 'The Lord has hidden it from me!' (2 Kings 4:27). In other words, 'I don't know.'"[2]

Cooke goes on to say, "Oddly enough, a prophecy will give us positive highlights about our future role or tasks, but may say nothing about any pitfalls we may encounter. It may not refer to enemy opposition, people letting us down, or any crushing disappointments that we may experience as we attempt to be faithful to our call."[3]

God may give us a little bit here and a little bit there. In retrospect, we may wonder why God didn't tell us this or that, or why He did tell us some seemingly unimportant detail. God always knows what He is doing when He reveals His heart to us through prophecy. That is something that we must simply trust. We must bear in mind, however, that we do not know all we may encounter, or how the prophecies may be fulfilled. Prophecy may point out a path, but we must follow the Lord daily and trust in Him as we move ahead along that path. Prophetic fulfillment comes in moving down the path that was pointed out through personal prophecy.

Prophecy Evolves

As we follow the Lord in obedience, He will give us our next piece. He will not tell us what He wants us to do three steps down the road. He gives it to us step by step. Such was the case with Abraham. God gave him a piece here and a piece there. Each time Abraham obeyed, God would speak to him again. God would confirm, expand, give new insights, and move Abraham on to his next place. One exciting dimension of Abraham's prophetic evolution comes in Genesis 22 when God reveals Himself as Jehovah Jireh to Abraham. This name of God actually means that God will reveal provision that we can't see, so we can advance into our future. Another tremendous concept in this chapter was that God prophesied the next piece of Abraham's destiny into his son Isaac. Therefore, what Abraham could not accomplish or complete was passed on to the next generation.

That is the way of prophecy. Each prophetic word is incomplete, yet as we are faithful to obey God, we receive new pieces of the puzzle. Prophecies will often build on earlier prophecies to bring confirmation and fresh understanding. Cooke writes, "The Lord will never speak the totality of his heart to us in a single prophetic word. Rather he speaks words that will give us a focus for now and the immediate future. As we work within those prophecies and allow our lives to be encouraged and shaped by them, we can see that prophecy builds from one word to another."[4]

Prophecy Is Conditional

The key to the process of prophecy is obedience. God will not usurp our wills and force us to follow His will. Mary, for instance, could have said no to the prophetic pronouncement that she would become pregnant. Instead, she responded by saying, "Behold the maidservant of the Lord! Let it be to me according to your word" (Luke 1:38). Had she said no, the Holy Spirit would never have forced her to become pregnant! Although she did not completely understand how this would happen, nor did she grasp the magnitude of what she had been chosen for, nevertheless, she knew that through the prophetic word, God had revealed His destiny for her life. Through her choice of obedience, the word came to pass and the human race gained access to its full redemptive plan.

The condition of obedience to the Holy Spirit is not a negotiable factor in prophetic fulfillment. In the Old Testament the word "faith" is used only twice. However, we find that the concept of faith is built in to the obedience of God's people based upon the promise that God has spoken to them. As these people obeyed, they became the fathers and mothers of our faith. Therefore, when God's word comes to you always look for the obedience factor.

Just because we have received a prophetic word does not mean it's a done deal. We are often tempted to believe that the fulfillment of a prophetic word is the next step in our lives, but there may be some things we have to do first in obedience to God. Abraham, for instance, had to be circumcised before he saw prophetic fulfillment. And then there was that big event where he had to put Isaac, his only son, on the altar. "Only son" meant that his entire future was wrapped up in this individual. However, that was the condition God had placed on him before He could reveal and extend His promise to the next generation.

Let us add one note of clarification: There is some prophecy that is unconditional and that God alone will fulfill. God is sovereign. He can do anything He wishes. But usually in His plan He has made it provisional for us to come into agreement with His sovereign hand. Therefore the words that He chooses to sovereignly accomplish are usually pertaining to the human race as a whole, rather than personal prophecy. This does not remove His sovereign grace to intervene at any time in our life, but it keeps us actively pursing Him.

Prophecy Has Timing

We must understand the seasons of God and not move out of His timing. Not every prophetic word is given in a *now* time. The prophecy that Daniel uncovered for the children of Israel had to lie dormant for 70 years before its time came!

One of the first prophetic words that ever came over my life was "You will have an anointing to know God's times and seasons. You will move supernaturally in His timing." I had no idea what this word meant. If there has been one anointing God has taught me in my life, it's this one. This anointing has been called by many the Issachar Anointing (see 1 Chron. 12:32).

Receiving a word about a future ministry might not mean that we run off and start moving in that direction the next day. In misplaced enthusiasm, many people might start doing what they were eventually supposed to do, but because they moved out of God's season, they will never be as effective as if they had waited on the Lord. It is like a baby who is born prematurely. That child may be alive but will have many more weaknesses, complications, and developmental obstacles to overcome, and may never reach the potential it would have had if it had been carried to full term. We need to be sensitive to God's development—of training, mentoring and circumstances in our lives that will provide the fertile soil where prophetic fulfillment will blossom to its fullest.

By the same token, we need to know when to move with a prophetic word. When I first met Rebecca Sytsema, she was single. She had promises from the Lord about her husband but had not yet met him. In 1994 several of us were preparing to go to a spiritual warfare conference. Rebecca shared with me she had had a dream that she was going to meet her husband at that conference. I immediately knew that was right. We got on the phone to make her a hotel reservation, but the receptionist told us there was no room available.

Without hesitation I said to the hotel worker, "You must find her a room! Her husband is waiting for her there!" Without any explanation of what I meant by my statement, the people at the hotel were able to find a room. It was at that conference that Rebecca met Jack Sytsema. Two years later I performed their wedding ceremony, and they have since had three children and are on a solid path toward all that God has for them in their lives. But what if she had not gone to the conference? I can't say that she would never have met Jack, but she would have missed a *now* season and had to wait longer than God intended to move toward prophetic fulfillment.

This should give great encouragement to those waiting on a similar promise. God has the times and seasons worked out. Do not run ahead of God, but be prepared to move when the time comes!

THE DANGERS OF PRESUMPTION

Besides moving out of God's timing, there are other dangers we can encounter with personal prophecy if we move in presumption. In other words, we receive a prophecy and, rather than allowing the Lord to work it out in our lives, we presume we know exactly what the prophecy means and try to make it happen. The word may be accurate, but the interpretation can get us moving in the wrong direction. Jesus overcame the spirit of presumption in the wilderness. Satan would quote Scripture to Him and try and get Him to act on it. But Jesus defied Satan's attempts to get Him moving out of God's timing.

The enemy does not care which end of the continuum he uses to get you into unbelief. He can use doubt and hardness of heart to keep you from moving forward, or he can use presumption to get you to move forward out of season. When we move in presumption, we open up ourselves and our families to needless attacks from the enemy. We need to be careful not to presume when and how God intends to bring prophetic fulfillment. We must remember that we only see a part of the picture. The way to avoid the pitfall of presumption is to obey the Lord in what you know you need to do next. In her book *The Voice of God*, Cindy Jacobs offers the following list of questions to help us stay out of presumption when we are ready to make changes based on a word or prophecy:

- Is this consistent with everything God has been saying about my life?
- How will this affect my current responsibilities? For example, will I be able to take care of my family financially? What kind of stress will this put on my family? Are they willing to sacrifice what will be required if I make these changes in my life?
- Have I reached a maturity level in my life that will enable me to perform with integrity the new tasks and/or changes, or will I flake out because I am not properly prepared?

• Do brothers and sisters in the Lord witness to this word, especially those in authority over me?[5]

GOING TO WAR

Having given some basic issues that are important for us to understand when it comes to personal prophecy, let's look at the spiritual warfare often necessary to see prophecy fulfilled. Just as God has a plan for your life, you can be just as sure that Satan also has a plan for your life. Satan considers it his job to thwart every plan and purpose God has for you, for your family and for your territory. That is the very essence of spiritual warfare—whose plan will prevail?

> Timothy, my son, I give you this instruction in keeping with the prophecies once made about you, so that by following them you may fight the good fight, holding on to faith and a good conscience. Some have rejected these and so have shipwrecked their faith (1 Tim. 1:18-19, *NIV*).

Do you have a prophetic promise concerning your children, but they are not making wise choices? Do you have prophetic promises concerning ministry, finances, future direction, barrenness breaking off your life, or any number of other things? Keeping in mind all we have discussed in this chapter concerning obedience, timing, presumption and prophetic evolution, ask the Lord if the enemy is at work to keep you from prophetic fulfillment. If so, it's time to go to war! As Jim Goll puts it, "Once you have secured an authentic prophetic promise, load it, take aim and shoot! Fight the fight and wage war with the prophetic."[6]

PRAYING A PROPHETIC WORD

God's word has tremendous power. Remember that it was by His word alone that He created light: "Then God *said*, 'Let there be light'; and there was light" (Gen. 1:3, emphasis added). By His word alone He created day and night, the earth and the heavens, land and sea, vegetation and every living creature. Everything that has been created exists because of the word of God. Furthermore, we see in John 1 that Jesus is the Word of God, "In the beginning was the Word, and the Word was with God, and the Word was God. And the Word became flesh and dwelt among us, and we beheld His glory, the glory as of the only begotten of the Father, full of grace and truth" (John 1:1,14). God's Word, therefore, not only gives us our being but also provides our redemption and secures our future through Christ.

When God speaks a prophetic promise, there is power within the words. There is power to gain the supply we need. There is power to step into a new level of faith. And there is power to overthrow the enemy. Couple with that the fact that our own words have a certain measure of power in them. Our words have the power to both bless and curse (see Jas. 3:9). Proverbs 18:21 reads that life and death are in the power of the tongue. Our words spoken in prayer can move the very hand of God and can block Satan's destructive maneuvers. Therefore, when we take a prophetic word that God has given us and speak it back to God in prayer, it is a potent combination.

Jim Goll reminds us, "At times we must declare the [prophetic] word to our circumstances and any mountain of opposition standing in the way. We remind ourselves of the promise that lies ahead, and we remind the devil and command any foul spirits—for example, the spirit of discouragement—to back off, declaring what the written and spoken promises of God reveal.

Each of us has purposes, promises and a destiny to find, fight for and fulfill. So take your 'Thus saith the Lord' to battle with you and fight."[7]

WHAT ARE WE WARRING AGAINST?

There are five areas we see from the Word of God where we are in conflict:

The devil. Satan and his demons affect most of us. This includes Christians. He has a hierarchy and a horde underneath him that are confederated to stop the purposes of God.

1. **The flesh.** The flesh tries to hang on for dear life instead of submitting to the power of the cross and being crucified. Galatians 5:24 reads we should crucify our flesh each day. The flesh hinders us from obeying God. Without this daily crucifixion, we give the devil the right to tempt and ensnare us.

2. **Enemies.** Many times evil spirits will embed in individuals or groups of individuals collectively. Then they use these individuals to set themselves against God's covenant plan in a person's life.

3. **The world.** The world system is organized and is usually competing contrary to God's will. We are enemies of the world. The god of this world is controlling the world system. Though we are not part of this world's system, we still live in it. The world system has both a religious aspect as well as a governmental aspect that must be understood if we are going to successfully maneuver in the world but never be part of the world.

4. **Death.** Death is our final enemy. Jesus overcame death and we must war with the strategies of death until we have completed our life cycle on the earth. And through His Spirit we can also overcome.

If we do not war these things, we will never possess the inheritance God has given us.

A WAR STRATEGY

Because of what we are warring against, we must have a war strategy for our life. In addition to the power of praying a prophetic word back to God, the Bible has many other warfare strategies when it comes to prophetic fulfillment. One excellent example of this is in 2 Chronicles 20. In this story a number of Judah's enemies came together to form a confederation against Judah and were planning to invade their God-ordained, God-promised boundaries. In obedience to the Lord, Judah had not previously invaded those who were in the confederation and who were now arising to steal what rightfully belonged to Judah. There was no question that the combined strength of their enemies could easily have overthrown them.

Jehoshaphat, who was a godly king, cried out to the Lord for a strategy for the warfare they faced. As he addressed the people he said, "Believe in the LORD your God, and you shall be established; believe His prophets, and you shall prosper" (2 Chron. 20:20). He called the nation together and followed these steps:

1. **They fasted** (v. 3). One of the greatest weapons we have in spiritual warfare is fasting. In *Possessing Your Inheritance* we said, "Fasting is a discipline that most

religions and cults understand because this sacrifice releases power. For the Christian, fasting is essential. Often you cannot gain the revelation you need for your next step without it. . . . Fasting removes spiritual clutter and positions us to receive from God. By fasting, we make it possible for the Lord to more powerfully reveal Himself to us—not because He speaks more clearly when we fast, but because we can hear Him more clearly."[8]

2. **They inquired of the Lord** (v. 4). This was a strategy David often used when he was about to be overthrown by his enemies. Each time David inquired of the Lord, he received strategic revelation that led to victory. Like David and like the people of Judah, when we are at war and we inquire of the Lord, we should expect Him to answer in a way that will provide strategy and direction for us.

3. **In faith they declared their God-given boundaries reminding God of His promises of inheritance to them** (v. 7). As we described above, they prayed the prophecy back to God, and they did so in faith. They let their faith arise. Faith is that pause between knowing what God's plan is and seeing it actually take place.[9] According to Jim Goll, "Take any promises that have been spoken to you by the Holy Spirit and turn them into persistent prayer, reminding God of His word. . . . Use these confirmed, authentic words from heaven to create faith within your heart. Let them pave the way for the entrance of ever-increasing faith in your life."[10]

4. **They acknowledged their own futility and recognized that they needed to keep their eyes on God**

or be overtaken by the enemy (v. 12). Even though we may feel powerless and helpless in the face of Satan's onslaughts, we need to remember that our perspective is very different from God's. If we focus purely on our circumstances, Satan can use what we see with our eyes to bring discouragement, hopelessness, rob our joy, and cause us to be overtaken by fear. But when we keep our eyes on the Lord, we can transcend our circumstances by quieting our hearts and minds and focusing on the Lord and His promises. Psalm 25:15 reads, "My eyes are ever toward the LORD, for He shall pluck my feet out of the net."

5. **They positioned themselves to face the enemy** (v. 17). Positioning is a crucial element of any warfare. If we are not in position when the enemy comes, he can easily overtake us. We must, therefore, be sure that we are in full obedience to all the Lord has required of us, and that we are walking on the path He has set for us. Then, donning the full armor of God, we will be ready to face the enemy when he attacks. We, therefore, need to ask ourselves, *Are we standing where we need to be? Do we need to change course or direction to get into the right position?*

6. **They sought counsel** (v. 21). It is vitally important for us to be surrounded by those who can give us wise counsel. Satan is such a master of deception that if we are standing alone, we can easily fall into deception. I have often heard Cindy Jacobs say, "If you don't think you can be deceived, then you already are!" If you are not under spiritual authority to those who are wise in the ways of God and routinely asking for their counsel, ask the Lord to bring

you to that place before moving on in warfare.

7. **They worshiped and praised the Lord** (v. 22). There is, perhaps, no stronger weapon of warfare than praise and worship to the Lord. Satan hates our worship to God for many reasons. For one, he is jealous of our worship. He longs to obtain it for himself through whatever means he can. For another, he knows that the weapon of worship is strong and effective. Consider the words of Psalm 149:5-9:

> Let the saints be joyful in glory; let them sing aloud on their beds. Let the high praises of God be in their mouth, and a two-edged sword in their hand, to execute vengeance on the nations, and punishments on the peoples; to bind their kings with chains, and their nobles with fetters of iron; to execute on them the written judgment—this honor have all His saints. Praise the LORD!

Another important reason is explained by Cindy Jacobs, "When we praise God, He inhabits or enters our praises, and His power overwhelms the power of the enemy. He is a mighty God, and Satan cannot match His strength. Light will dispel the darkness through God's entering into our praise."[11] Through praise, the Lord Himself begins to do warfare on our behalf to silence our enemy, as we shall see.

THE VICTORY

In this story of Jehoshaphat we find the passage, "Stand still and see the salvation of the LORD" (2 Chron. 20:17). As the people of Judah earnestly sought the Lord and followed the strategy that He gave them, the Scripture says that they were to stand still and allow the Lord to battle on their behalf. In the end, it was the Lord who set ambushes against the enemy so that they were utterly destroyed. Verse 24 reads that not one of their enemies escaped!

The Lord will do the same for us. We must seek the Lord, be obedient to His commands, and let Him handle the rest for us: "'Not by might nor by power, but by My Spirit,' says the LORD of hosts" (Zech. 4:6). If we are to have prophetic fulfillment in our lives, we have no choice but to believe that God will do what He said he will do!

THE SPOILS OF WAR

This story does not end with the victory of the people of Judah against their enemies. There is something more that we need to grasp. Their victory was not complete until they gathered the spoils of war.

> When Jehoshaphat and his people came to take away their spoil, they found among them an abundance of valuables on the dead bodies, and precious jewelry, which they stripped off for themselves, more than they could carry away; and they were three days gathering the spoil because there was so much (2 Chron. 20:25).

Can you imagine so many dead bodies covered in so much wealth that it took the people of Judah a full three days to collect it all—and it was more than they could carry away? God saw to it that their enemy was not only destroyed but also that the spoils of war were far beyond what they ever expected! God did the same for the children of Israel as they were being set free from their captivity in Egypt. Scripture says the Egyptians loaded them up with articles of gold, silver and clothing after the Lord secured their freedom from slavery. Through the process of obeying God in the warfare, *God gave them much more than was in the original promise.* He not only secured the boundaries He had set for them but also caused them to gain wealth in the process.

As the Lord brings us into victory, we need to ask Him what spoils of war He has for us to gather. What has the enemy been holding from us that he must now give up as a result of our victory? In some cases it may be literal wealth. In other cases it may be salvation for our loved ones. It could be restoration of destroyed relationships. It could be a physical healing or deliverance from what has been tormenting us. No matter what spoils of war God has for us, we need to understand that the very nature of war is that the one who is defeated must relinquish something to the victor. Be sure that you have gathered all the spoils that the Lord has for you when you come into victory.

In addition to the wealth they gathered, the army of Judah was strengthened for future battles as they were able to gather the swords, shields and other weapons of war from their fallen enemies. This represents a new strength and a new anointing that comes in victory. As we gain each victory in the war over prophetic fulfillment, God releases a new anointing of authority on us that gives us even greater power to overthrow our enemy in the battles that lie ahead.

A TIME TO WAR AND A TIME TO REST

Ecclesiastes 3 reads that to everything there is a season, a time for every purpose under heaven: "a time for war" (v. 8, *NIV*)!

When it is a time for war, we must have a paradigm for war! The Church is being prepared to enter its most dynamic season of warfare, worship and harvest. When it is a time for war—WAR! David's greatest downfall came during his reign, when it was time to go to war and he stayed home. Passivity in a time of war is disastrous.

There are also times of rest. Not every season of our lives is meant to be marked by warfare. There is a time for everything, including rest. In fact, without seasons of rest, we will never be able to quiet our hearts long enough to hear the voice of the Lord, or to gain revelation for how we should move forward. We need to be wise about how the Lord intends to bring prophetic fulfillment into our lives.

Yes, there will be times of war when we need to stand up and fight. However, the enemy will attempt to prolong our seasons of warfare in order to rob us of our strength. God's grace covers our natural lack of strength during seasons of war. But when God is ready to move us on, we are no longer covered by the same measure of grace. We must never get so caught up in our warfare that we take our eyes off of the Lord, and that we do not enter into the rest He has for us so that we can continue moving forward.

Notes

1. Some of the material in this section has been adapted from Chuck D. Pierce and Rebecca Wagner Sytsema, *Receiving the Word of the Lord* (Colorado Springs, CO: Wagner Publications, 1999), pp. 24-25.
2. Graham Cooke, *Developing Your Prophetic Gifting* (Kent, England: Sovereign World, Ltd., 1994), p. 119.
3. Ibid., p. 120.
4. Ibid., p 123.
5. Cindy Jacobs, *The Voice of God* (Ventura, CA: Regal Books, 1995), p. 85.
6. Jim W. Goll, *Kneeling on the Promises* (Grand Rapids, MI: Chosen Books, 1999), p. 172.

7. Ibid., p. 173.
8. Chuck D. Pierce and Rebecca Wagner Sytsema, *Possessing Your Inheritance* (Ventura, CA: Renew, 1999), pp. 134-135.
9. Ibid., p. 23.
10. Goll, *Kneeling on the Promises*, p. 173.
11. Cindy Jacobs, *Possessing the Gates of the Enemy* (Tarrytown, NY: Chosen Books, 1991), p. 178.